Track Construction

Jeff Geary and John Shaw

KRB Publications
2 Denewulf Close
BISHOPS WALTHAM
Hants
SO32 1GZ

ISBN 0954203593

Printed by the Amadeus Press

Acknowledgements

I would very much like to thank all those who have taken the trouble to contact me with comments and suggestions following the release of the first book and in particular Ian McGibbon. I am also grateful to a number of friends who have passed on valuable information on track building, both prototype and model, and especially Graham Hatton, David Dere-Jones and David Yule. Finally to those who have allowed us to clamber all over their layouts at exhibitions and the like in order to obtain photographs and information. In particular in this area I would thank Dave Douglas of the Manchester Model Railway Club, Gordon Gravett, Ian Hopkins, Philip Morgan and Denis Tillman.

Jeff Geary, Whitchurch, 2003.

Important Note

The Trax computer program contained within this book is supplied as part of the book and CD ROM package. It is intended solely for the use of the purchaser and is not to be lent, hired, copied or stored in any other form other than as originally supplied. Whilst every care has been taken in the production of the program, neither KRB Publications nor the author can accept any responsibility whatsoever for any damage caused by use of this program. By opening the sealed package containing the CD ROM the purchaser agrees to accept these conditions.

Contents

Introduction

Following the success of *Wiring the Layout,* and encouraged by Kevin Robertson, I have produced a second volume which, I hope, will be of interest and value to modellers in all scales. Whereas the previous volume focussed on the electrical side of the hobby, the present book is about building track. I have been fortunate to have obtained the help of my friend John Shaw, who has built more track than most! He has certainly built a lot more than me, so his contribution of the three 'practical' chapters (3, 4 and 5) is of enormous benefit.

I have also produced a new *Trax* program on a CD to go with this book. *Trax2* will accept all the layout files that you created with *Trax1*. It will recognize the electrical information you created, although the present volume does not go into the implementation of feeds, breaks, control etc. *Trax2,* however, gives you templates in profusion. In virtually every scale and gauge combination, with different wheel and track standards, you can now print a template for almost any possible track formation.

As with *Wiring the Layout,* however, we must remind the reader that the CD is provided free with the book and is intended only to be used by the purchaser. It is not a commercially produced piece of software and is not supported by an army of software engineers. If you do find a bug, by all means let us know via the publisher, and we will do our best to correct it, but no guarantees! As with the handful of bugs found by readers of *Wiring the Layout,* it is intended that corrections will be posted as available on the KRB Publications web site at www.kevinrobertsonbooks.co.uk.

Jeff Geary

What we all try and emulate in miniature. The location is the east end of Manchester Victoria (L & Y) and whilst the period and location may not be to everyone's choice the importance of accurate track planning, building and laying cannot be over-emphasised if good running is to be achieved. It also matters not what scale you are working in, hence the principles referred to in the text can apply from the smallest to largest scale and layout.

Chapter 1

TRACK DESIGN

The art of designing a track plan, as with so many aspects of the model railway hobby, is the art of compromise. The modeller must attempt to find a happy medium between a great many, often conflicting, requirements. In this chapter, we review some of the steps involved in arriving at a suitable design. There are few hard and fast rules - it is all very much up to individual preferences.

To help the reader through the design process, a computer program *Trax2*, is included on the CD that comes with this book. This includes a number of facilities to assist with both the design and construction of track, as we shall see shortly.

What Type of Track Plan?

There are several alternative schemes for the design of a track plan. It could be a continuous run, say an oval or circle, or a more ambitious shape such as a figure of eight. A continuous run tends to occupy a lot of space because the curves cannot be too tight. However, it does have the benefit that trains can be set running, and the operator can sit back and relax watching the trains go by. Part of the continuous run can be set aside for storage sidings or loops so that several different trains can be held ready for action.

Alternatively, the track plan could be of the end-to-end type, where trains basically run up and down a straight baseboard. Such a layout can usually be fitted into a smaller space. The most common end-to-end scheme has a terminus station at one end of the run, whilst at the other is a 'fiddle yard', where trains are assembled to run into the station. Because the fiddle yard is generally not regarded as part of the scenic area of the layout, this assembly can be done by hand shunting. Once out of the fiddle yard and onto the model proper, however, the train should be worked as closely as possible to the real thing.

At a terminus this would involve a steam engine running round a passenger train, so as to be at the front for the return journey. If it were a tender engine then it might also need turning on a turntable or triangle. Goods trains would have to be shunted so that wagons end up in their appropriate locations, such as coal staithes, cattle pens, side and end loading bays and so on. For the return journey, the wagons would need to be reassembled in proper sequence. There might well be rules to be observed here, such as cattle wagons travelling next to the engine, there having to be at least two barrier wagons between the engine and an inflammable load such as a petrol tanker, and, of course, the brake van must be at the end. Care needs to be taken at the track planning stage that all necessary moves are possible, that sidings are of adequate length, and that tracks are sufficiently far apart, especially on the tighter curves, so that vehicles on adjacent tracks do not collide.

Instead of the fiddle yard, you might opt to have two terminus stations, and run traffic between them This makes for a lot of operational interest, but tends to make it difficult to have a large amount of stock. The beauty of a fiddle yard is that many trains can be packed together in a relatively small space, so allowing a greater variety on the layout. With two terminus stations, all of the trains are visible at all times. If there are too many of these, it may look a little unrealistic.

Fig 1.1 - Copper clad sleepers and soldered trackwork on part of the Manchester Model Railway Society's superb 'Dewsbury Midland' layout - a continuous run in fine scale OO.

Fig 1.2, left - view of MMRS storage sidings/loops. The track was built by Dave Douglas using SMP 75 rail and copperclad sleepers.

Fig 1.3, lower left -Fig 1.3 - Chris Hatton operating Ian Hopkin's 'St George's Hill' - a fine scale 7mm terminus with fiddle yard based on 19th century South Western practice. The whole occupies a space not much more than 8 feet long. When packed for transport it fits neatly into its unusual storage case inside the specially constructed clock!

Instead of a terminus, you might want to model a through station with a fiddle yard at each end. This permits an even greater number of different trains, but has the disadvantage that a smaller proportion of the total length of the model is scenic. A useful idea that many layout designers have adopted is to hide the fiddle yard behind something with scenic or operational interest that occupies only a narrow strip of the baseboard. A shunting spur or a private siding might fulfil this purpose, with either a painted backscene or a factory building modelled in low-relief to hide the fiddle yard from view.

Prototype or Freelance?

Hand in hand with the above, you will need to decide whether the model is to be a true-to-scale reproduction of a particular location at a particular period, or whether it is to be entirely fictitious. Between these two extremes, there are a whole variety of different possibilities. Your model might seek to represent a particular station, trying to capture as much of its atmosphere and appearance as possible, whilst making some compromises to fit it into available space. Alternatively, you might want to build a model which is based on a particular railway company's practice

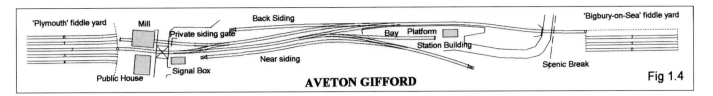

Fig 1.4 - Aveton Gifford - a through station with 2 fiddle yards.

but is not of an actual station that existed. For example, "What Aveton Gifford station might have looked like had the railway ever reached that town".

If you are building a model of a particular prototype, then unless the layout is a very simple one indeed, the space available will almost always be too small. Compromises must then be made in areas such as platform sizes, number of sidings, length of run-round loops and so on.

The traditional way of testing out these compromises is to use a pencil and paper and sketch out various possibilities until one is decided upon that comes closest to the individual modellers taste. Unfortunately, in this regard a pencil and paper can be extremely deceptive! The modeller can very easily be convinced that a particular track plan will fit into a given area, because the appropriate number of points, crossings etc can be shoe-horned in. However, there are many other factors that may not have been considered. If the turnouts of two points have to be joined by a section of curved track, what will be its radius? It is easy to draw what looks like a reasonable curve which, when it actually comes to building the layout, turns out to have an excruciatingly small radius if its ends are to truly line up with the point turnouts. If

two sidings lead from a point, and are drawn with a length of two feet, do not expect to be able to use their whole length. As we get closer to the point, the sidings will get closer to each other, and collisions will occur if vehicles are parked too close. With a pencil and paper, the modeller may be tempted to draw the point with a rather sharper angle, thereby being deluded into thinking the sidings will hold more.

The *Trax2* program will help you avoid these pitfalls, by ensuring that all of the joins in your track components do truly line up. It will also alert you to especially tight curves, and will allow you to project onto your track plan the clearance lines that correspond to a vehicle of maximum width. When you get *Trax2* to join up two loose ends with a piece of flexible track, it will ensure that the resulting curves have the necessary common tangency (discussed in the next chapter) and so forth. To illustrate this, let us follow through an example layout design using the *Trax2* program.

A Country Terminus

For the example, we shall design a single-line branch terminus station. However, unlike the vast majority of such examples, ours will *not* be on the GWR! For a change, and because

operationally it was much more interesting, we shall take an example from up north - Holcombe Brook station at the end of the branch line from Bury on the old Lancashire and Yorkshire Railway.

One of the authors spent much time in his childhood at Holcombe Brook, where his Aunty Mary had a cottage on nearby Holcombe Hill. This is a famous local landmark, with the splendid Holcombe Tower at the summit, a monument to Sir Robert Peel who was born in the area. It would make a fine painted backscene. Although only a single track, the line was busy. The 1905 working timetable showed around 30 trains a day in each direction, and there was much of operational interest, 5 goods trains, light engine workings to provide a shunting engine during the middle of the day, and so on. There were some local rules which allowed for some unusual workings, for example the propelling of wagons (*without* a brake van) up the 1 in 40 gradient into Holcombe Brook from further down the line. The interested reader is referred to the excellent booklet by David Westall and published by the Lancashire & Yorkshire Railway Society (ISSN 0261-7919).

The prototype track plan, as it was in 1908, is shown in figure 1.5. It was a

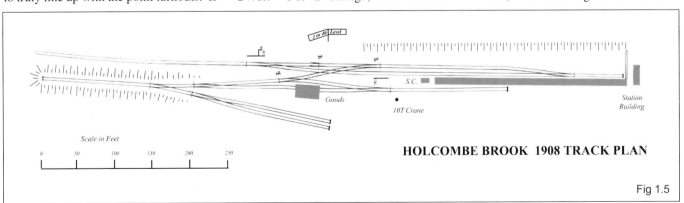

HOLCOMBE BROOK 1908 TRACK PLAN

Fig 1.5

Holcombe Brook in April 1951. The view is looking towards what would have been the sector-plate engine release. It is interesting how the prototype would have operated this. For once it is a case of on a model it is easier!

Harold D. Bowtell.

fairly typical layout for a single track terminus station, and would not have been out of place on a great many railways. The line entered the station area up a very steep (1 in 40) incline. There was a single platform with the station building at right angles to it, just beyond the retaining wall at the end of the line. A loop allowed the engine to detach from its train and run round to the other end. Unusually, the platform road itself was reached via a right-hand turnout, the straight on route being into the loop. The layout was altered in later years to a more conventional scheme with the point re-aligned to give platform access via the straight on setting.

Because there were so many passenger trains, it would not have been convenient to use the platform loop in shunting activities. Therefore, a second loop was available in the goods yard, which was accessed via a trailing point in the run-round loop. The goods shed was built on the loop, and a 10-ton crane was placed nearby. A headshunt with a pair of sidings off was built up on an embankment, so that it was at the same level as the rest of the yard, the ground falling off at 1 in 40 to either side of it. Note the sidings are arranged close together. This was a common feature; larger goods yards would have sidings arranged in pairs like this, with a wider space between the pairs for road vehicle access.

From the modeller's point of view, an interesting historical aside is that the original drawing for the station shows a sector plate at the end of the platform, rather than a point and a short spur for the engine to run onto the loop. The sector plate was never built, however if it were used on a model, it would save the length of a point.

Signalling was conventional. A pair of home signals controlled access to the platform road and the run-round loop, goods trains entering on the latter, and a starter signal was placed at the end of the platform. Three miniature signals controlled access to the main line from the loop, from the loop to the goods yard, and from yard to loop. These signals should ideally control the supply of electrical power to the appropriate sections of track, so that until the signal controlling a movement was reversed the engine would not be able to move. Methods of doing this are described in *Wiring The Layout.*

Designing the Model - First Attempt

The scale on figure 1.5 shows that Holcombe Brook was not a large station, so it should be possible to build a model of it in a relatively small area. Let us suppose we have 16 feet available, and want to model the station at 7mm to the foot (0 gauge). We shall first try to design the model using conventional 1 in

6 left- and right-hand points and a standard 1 in 6 diamond crossing.

It is advisable to start off with the trickiest part of the track plan, it being easier to fit the more straightforward parts in with this, than vice versa. We therefore start with the points and crossing forming the access from the main platform loop to the goods yard. Start up *Trax2*, select File|New, and set a layout size of 16 feet by 2 feet. Do not forget the units - if you type 16ft or 16' *Trax2* will know you mean feet. Numbers without units are taken to be millimetres, so if you just type 16, *Trax2* will object that this is too small for a layout in 0 gauge! Position two left-hand points and a diamond crossing on the layout, then join them up as shown in figure 1.6 (step 1). To join track parts, use the joining tool (a small black arrow with a plus sign on the 'track' toolbar). Click first on the end of the piece of track you want to stay put, then click the end of a piece of track you want to move to join onto it. In this case, you will want to position the left-hand point adjacent to the goods shed first. Use the move tool (a hand) to place this. Then join up the diamond and second point as in the figure. Note that once you have joined them up, the move tool operates on all of them as a unit.

Add a straight and set its length to 4' 6" (right-click the straight and select 'Properties'), then add a right-hand point,

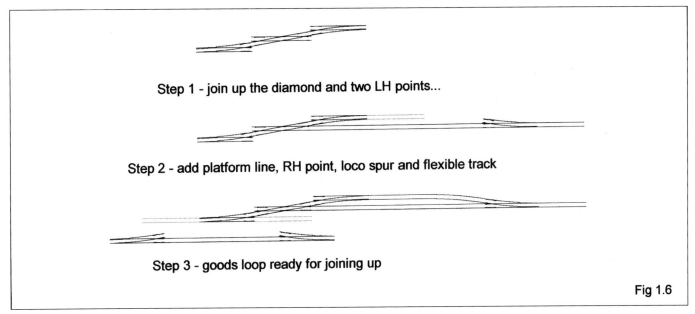

Step 1 - join up the diamond and two LH points...

Step 2 - add platform line, RH point, loco spur and flexible track

Step 3 - goods loop ready for joining up

Fig 1.6

a 1' 3" straight for the loco spur, and join them up as in figure 1.6 (step 2). If your loco spur protrudes over edge of the layout, use the move tool to drag everything back onto the baseboard. You will notice that there is a dotted track attached to the point in the run-round. This is a piece of flexible track, shown as a wiggly dotted line on the 'track' toolbar. This can be joined in the usual way to the point as shown. With the joining tool, click its free end, then the unattached end of the right-hand point. *Trax2* will now work out that to join the two fixed locations, it needs a certain length of straight and a curve of a certain radius. It will create these, and join them up to complete the loop. This feature can save a lot of time in drawing track plans, and also ensures that all parts are joined up with geometric precision.

In a similar fashion, proceed to construct the goods loop, positioning first a 3' straight, then the left and right-hand points and flexible track to join up to the existing trackwork. Figure 1.6 (step 3) shows this process nearing completion. With a little practice, you will find that you can create a whole track plan in a matter of minutes, and the end result will be something like figure 1.7. You may well make a mistake; a common one is to click the wrong piece first when you are using the joining tool,

and cause the whole track plan jump out of place! If you do make a mistake, then you can 'undo' your error if you immediately click 'Undo' on the edit menu, or press Ctrl and Z on the keyboard. Another useful idea is to save your work frequently and change its name slightly each time, so that if you make a whole series of changes that you later decide you don't like, you can go back several stages.

Analysing the Layout

Once the track plan is to your liking, you can use *Trax2* to do some analysis on it. For example, if you open the Parts List dialog box (Tools menu) you can select a 'list type' of 'Sharp Curves'. This will reveal just how sharp *Trax2* has had to make some of the curves in order to join up the parts as you have indicated. In all probability some of these will be very sharp indeed, as short lengths of track have been bent around to join points etc. Also on the Tools menu, you will find a Minimum Radius dialog box, which will help you determine whether a wagon of a given wheelbase will be able to get round such curves. There will be more on this subject in the next chapter.

Another useful tool to help you analyse your track plan is on the Options menu, or can be activated by pressing F4.

This is the option to show clearance lines. These are generally shown as red dashed lines either side of each length of track. They represent 9 ft 6 ins (the typical maximum vehicle width) at the appropriate scale for the layout you have set up. Where lines converge, for example as they approach a point, you will find that at some point the clearance lines intersect. This represents the point beyond which vehicles cannot be parked if you are to avoid collisions. Using this tool, you can determine whether your platform is long enough to accommodate the type of passenger train you wish to run, how much of your siding length is actually usable for wagon storage etc. One word of caution - a long vehicle on a sharp curve will have a substantial overhang, which will increase its effective width on the inside of the curve. You may need to make allowance for this adjacent to very sharp curves.

The track plan we have now produced can be built entirely from left and right hand points and one diamond crossing. It would be perfectly possible to make it from off-the-shelf proprietary track components. However, a critical eye cast over figure 1.5 and then figure 1.7 would reveal that the latter, although it has pretty much the same track plan, is less pleasing to the eye. The preponderance of straight parallel lines, the sudden

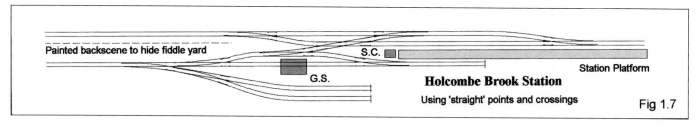

changes in radius and the identical appearance of all the points gives the layout something of the appearance of a toy train set rather than a model railway. Let us therefore consider an alternative approach.

Designing the Model - Second Attempt

Most railway lines comprised a series of very gentle curves, and these tend to look a lot more pleasing than straight lines. Long lengths of dead straight track tend to make boring models, in the opinion of the authors at least. In figure 1.8, we have shown an alternative approach, based on a long,

gentle curve rather than a straight. We have also allowed the curve of the line of the track to dictate the radius of the points, rather than vice versa. This means that we can eliminate the vast majority of the sharp radii that detract from the appearance of figure 1.7. Notice, for example, how the line of the goods loop round the back of the shed is smoother and how the sidings flow from the point in gentle, parallel curves rather than a series of bends and straights.

To achieve this, we have used two essential tools on the *Trax2* tool bar. These are the spacer tool and the alignment tool. The spacer is simply a

means of positioning the ends of two lengths of track a given distance apart and with the same orientation. This ensures that any parts joined up to them will be parallel. Once the spacer has been used to position the two tracks, it should be deleted. The alignment tool allows the ends of two or more lengths of track to be aligned in the same position and direction. In effect, they are superimposed on the track plan. Of course, this is physically impossible in reality, but its usefulness is that it allows us to line up, say, two curves in a similar fashion to a curved point using flexible track. We could then take the radius measurements

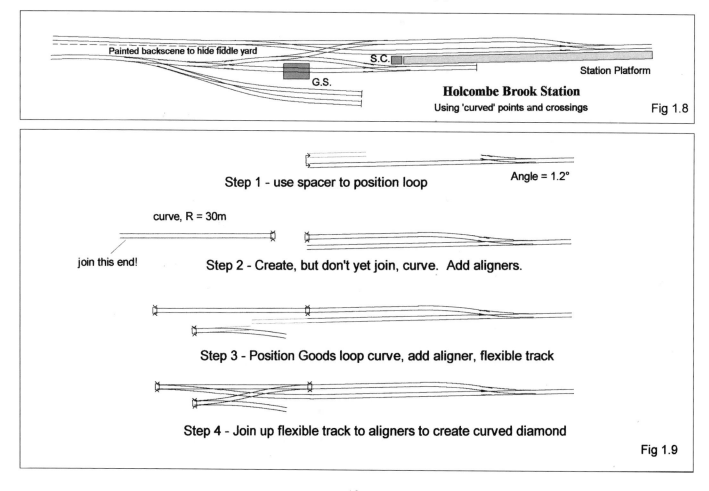

of the two curves and use these to create a custom curved point to fit a particular location in a track plan. This would then be substituted for the two individual curves. In this respect, the alignment tool is being used as a method of quickly working out what radii we need for a curved point in a given situation.

Another use of the alignment tool is to allow us to design a piece of trackwork that would otherwise not be within the capability of the *Trax2* program. For example, in figure 1.8, notice that the diamond crossing now has curved tracks. The program itself has built-in capability only to calculate the geometry for diamonds with straight tracks. However, by using the alignment tool, we can at least produce the rail profiles for a crossing with curves. Figure 1.9 illustrates how we created this part of the layout. Similar methods can be used to create even more complex track formations such as scissors crossings (straight or curved), four and even five way points, etc.

Track-building Methods and Materials

There are several possible methods of building track. Each has its own advantages and disadvantages, and the modellers must decide which best suits the particular situation.

Firstly, there is the copper-clad sleeper method, figure 1.10. Here, sleepers are made from copper-clad board made for printed circuit production. This consists of a sheet of fibre glass onto which is glued a thin film of copper. When used in a printed circuit, the copper film is etched away where no conducting path is needed, and components are soldered to the remaining copper. For use as sleepers, the board is cut into strips of standard sleeper length and width (8'6" by 10" on the prototype) and the rail is soldered to it at appropriate intervals. Note that the sleepers must be 'gapped', that is, they have a section of copper conductor removed in the centre to prevent short circuits between the rails.

Copper-clad construction is quick and relatively easy to build. Soldering is an extremely firm way of holding the rail in position, and it is perfectly possible to hold a section of rail firm with just one or two solder joints. Fibre glass board can be bought ready cut to the appropriate width and is cheap. One problem that can occur, however, is that if joints are resoldered a few times, or if too hot a soldering iron is used, the copper can lift away from the board. Another disadvantage of copper-clad construction is that there are no chairs on the sleepers. These can be added as cosmetic 'extras', although from a distance their necessity may be thought debatable. Look, for instance, at the beautiful trackwork in figure 1.1, Page 5, which is built using copper-clad sleepers without chairs.

A more recent development is the appearance of plastic sleepers and chairs plus the ability to hold these firmly together using one of the solvent type adhesives, figure 1.11. These actually dissolve the plastic, then evaporate away

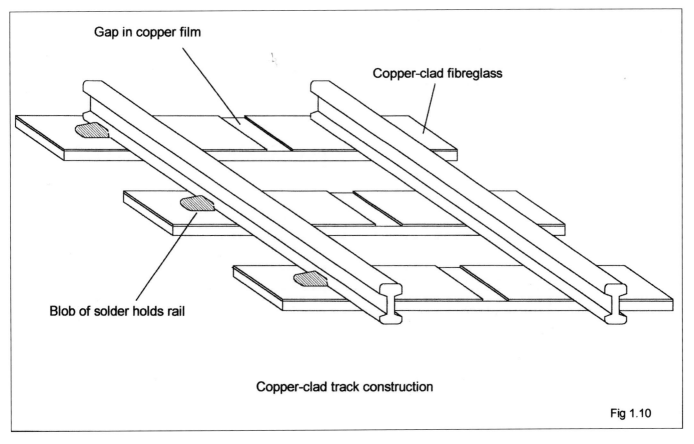

Gap in copper film

Copper-clad fibreglass

Blob of solder holds rail

Copper-clad track construction

Fig 1.10

leaving the two components firmly 'welded' together. Chairs suitable for a variety of different railway companies are available, and can give your trackwork a very authentic appearance. Plastic chairs can be purchased with the appropriate 1 in 20 inclination to hold the rails at the correct angle (see the next chapter for details). On the other hand, plastic is easily melted, if insufficient care is taken with the soldering of wires to rails and so on. The plastic chairs hold the rails less firmly than a solder joint. If it is necessary to support a short length of rail, for example a check rail, on only a small number of sleepers, it is not going to be held so firmly in position as with copper-clad.

If you do not like the appearance of plastic sleepers, you can use wooden ones. The same solvent cement that is used for plastic sleepers can be equally effective if it is used to soak a wooden sleeper, then the chair is held in position whilst the solvent evaporates. One way

of avoiding the sloppiness associated with holding short lengths of rail in plastic chairs is to solder the rail to brass rivets in the sleepers, and to add the chairs purely as cosmetic extras. This, of course, can only be done with wooden sleepers, as plastic ones would melt.

You can also obtain brass chairs, which are useful in conjunction with copper-clad sleepers. These allow you to combine the realism of chaired track with the strength of soldered joints. For example, the majority of a point can be built with plastic chairs and sleepers; then at crucial positions, where the rail needs holding firmly, one or two copper-clad sleepers can be used, with brass chairs soldered to the sleeper and rail.

As with all things, it is largely down to individual preference. If the modeller feels that the end result merits the time and effort put into construction, then by all means give your trackwork the full treatment. If, on the other hand, your track is merely a place to run your trains,

then you might not want to spend too much of your valuable modelling time on getting every last detail to perfection Both authors, it should be said, take a fairly pragmatic view of track construction. In making the inevitable choices and compromises, we tend to favour track that looks reasonably good without necessarily being an exact replica of a particular prototype, but that overall works well without derailments. The general principles adopted will be adequate for most modellers; however for those determined to model faithfully a particular railway company, specialist books are available to advise you on the types of chair to use, sleeper spacings, lengths of check rails and so on.

We shall look later in this book at the details of track construction. First, however, we review in the next chapter some of the key principles of track geometry, to ensure that our trains run reliably.

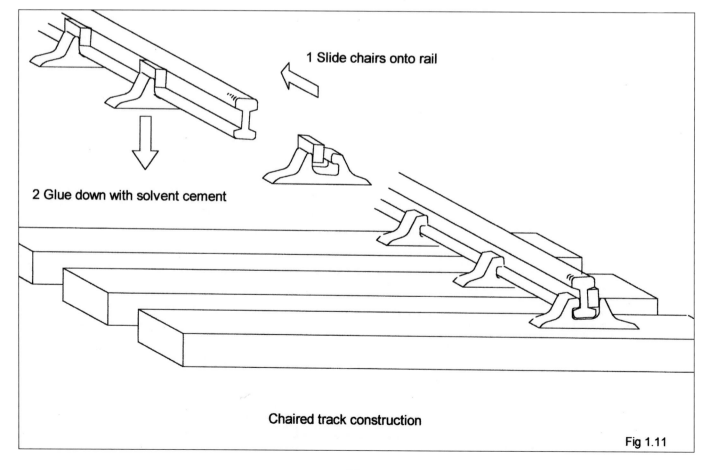

1 Slide chairs onto rail

2 Glue down with solvent cement

Chaired track construction

Fig 1.11

Chapter 2

TRACK GEOMETRTY

Reliability, one of the most important attributes of a well-built railway, is in large part a result of ensuring that the track geometry obeys some straightforward rules. If your track is laid in a haphazard fashion, then derailments will be inevitable. In this chapter, we review some of the geometrical principles that good trackwork should follow, and show how to ensure that the track you build conforms to these requirements.

As was mentioned in the previous chapter, *Trax2* has been extended to include facilities useful to track builders. Among these extensions is the ability to print full-size templates, including sleeper spacing, track breaks, check rails and clearance lines for a whole range of standard formations such as straight, curved and three-way points, diamonds, single and double slips, and more. Templates can be printed at any scale (4mm, 7mm, etc) or gauge (16.5mm, 18.83mm, 32mm, 33mm, etc), or indeed can be tailored to a scale and gauge dictated by the user.

In addition to these standard formations, as we have seen *Trax2* includes the ability to design your own track formation. For the advanced constructor, who has sufficient experience to work out sleeper positions and crossing details for him- or herself, this facility means that a template can be printed for almost any conceivable formation.

Plain Track

By plain track, we mean straights or curves which consist entirely of two running rails, held into *chairs* by means of a hardwood *key*. The chairs are in turn attached to *sleepers*. Figure 2.1 is an end-on view of a section through a length of plain track with a wagon or other vehicle standing upon it. The rail is shown shaded, and is of a profile known as *bullhead*, which was the most common type of rail prior to nationalisation. In later years, *flat-bottomed* rail has largely replaced bullhead. This has a much

Catch points were provided to prevent vehicles running back and otherwise fouling the running lines, note then the throw off is away from the main line. Detail such as the missing wooden key can make all the difference to the model. Arksey loops near Doncaster in 1951.

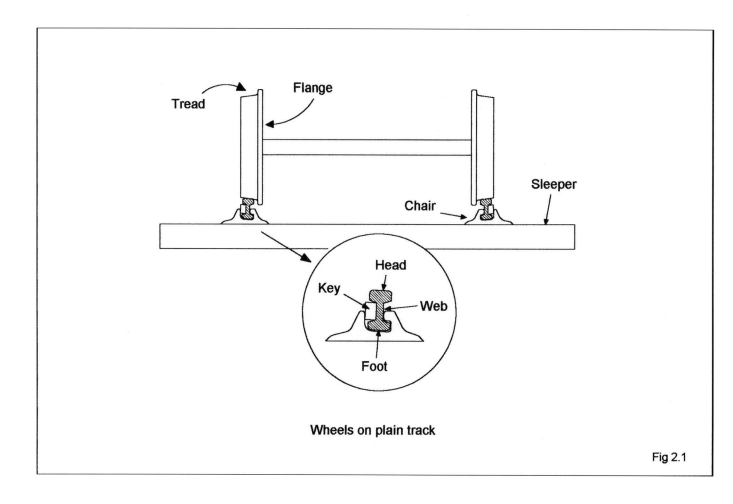

Wheels on plain track

Fig 2.1

wider and thinner foot than the bullhead variety. Both types of rail are available to the modeller, and you should investigate which type would be appropriate for the era of your model.

The wheels shown standing on the rail have a *flange* and a *tread*. Notice that the tread is coned, that is, it tapers slightly towards the outer face of the wheel. This taper is of vital importance to smooth running. On plain straight track, as shown, the coning ensures that the wheels sit centrally between the rails. Any tendency to the right or left would require lifting the centre of gravity of the vehicle, and would thus be opposed by its weight. Without a tapered tread, the wheel flanges would bounce to and fro between the inside faces of the rail head as the vehicle went along. These faces, incidentally, are known as the *running faces* of the rail, and their distance apart is known as the *gauge* of the track.

Notice also in figure 2.1 that the rails are inclined inwards to match the coning of the wheel tread. This inclination is 1 in 20, or about 3°. Proprietary chairs for track builders generally have this inclination built in, so that the modeller using these need not worry about reproducing it.

Round the Bend

When we come to curved track, the coning of the wheel tread fulfils a second and even more important function. One of the problems about taking a vehicle round a curve is that, for a given distance of travel round the centreline of the curve, the innermost wheel travels slightly less distance than the outer one. Without coning, this would mean that one or other of the treads would have to slip along the rail, since both wheels are firmly fixed to the same rotating axle. The frictional forces thus generated would use up some

of the motive power available. However, with coned treads, all that is necessary is that the wheels move slightly towards the outside of the curve.

In figure 2.2 (A), notice that the wheels have moved as a pair slightly to the right. This puts the tread of the left hand wheel in contact with the rail head a little nearer its outer face, and thus at a position where its circumference is slightly less. Conversely, the right hand wheel is in contact nearer the flange where the circumference is greater. This is exactly what we need if the rail is curving away to the left as we look at the figure. If it were curving to the right, the wheels would simply move in the opposite direction.

On the prototype, where curves are generally much less severe than on a model, this slight lateral movement is all that is required on gentle curves. However, on more pronounced curves

14

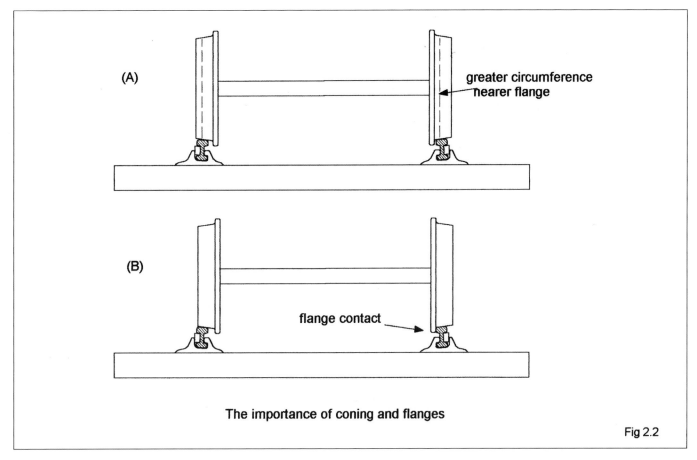

(A)

greater circumference
nearer flange

(B)

flange contact

The importance of coning and flanges

Fig 2.2

the coning is insufficient to take up all the differential movement required. At this point, the outermost flange will make contact with the running face of the rail, as in figure 2.2 (B), and the vehicle will now be guided round the bend by the flange. Unfortunately, this means considerable friction between flange and running face and is the principal reason for the fact that model trains run more slowly round curves than along the straight.

The amount of curve that can be accommodated by the coning alone is, in model terms, very little indeed. If you look at the 'Tools' menu of the *Trax* program you will find a 'Minimum Radius' calculator that, among other things, allows you to see how tight a curve can be negotiated without any flange contact at all. This is rather disappointingly large. For example, in 00 gauge it is nearly 13 feet.

Limiting Radius

As a curve gets tighter and tighter,

so the frictional forces become greater and the train will have more difficulty in negotiating the curve. Eventually, it will become physically impossible for the curve to be followed. To see why, we need to take a different viewpoint.

In figure 2.3 (A), we are looking sideways on at a vehicle on a length of track. Shown shaded is the effective part of the wheel flange, i.e. that which lies below the head of the rail. On straight track and very gentle curves, as we have seen, this will be held away from the actual running face by the action of gravity and the coning of the tread, as shown in plan view in figure 2.3 (B). When the vehicle enters a tight curve, as in figure 2.3 (C), the leading edge of the flange will make contact, and guide the vehicle around the bend, at the cost of a considerable increase in friction.

On a really tight bend, however, leading and trailing edges of the effective part of the inner and outer flanges will make contact with the running face of the

rail and the vehicle will be virtually locked up solid. This situation is illustrated in fig 2.3 (D). Any further reduction in curve radius, and the leading flange will climb over the outer rail, thus derailing the vehicle.

The radius at which this occurs is a complex function of several variables - the vehicle wheelbase (shorter vehicles can negotiate tighter curves), the wheel diameter (smaller wheels, likewise), the flange height and thickness, the distance apart of the wheels and the track gauge. All of these have a bearing on determining the result.

The *Trax* Minimum Radius Calculator allows you to set up all of these numerical values, then calculate the minimum radius that any particular vehicle will, in theory, go round. However, this minimum will only be achieved if every single measurement is spot-on, and if there are perfect running conditions - absolutely clean wheels and track, for instance, are essential. The

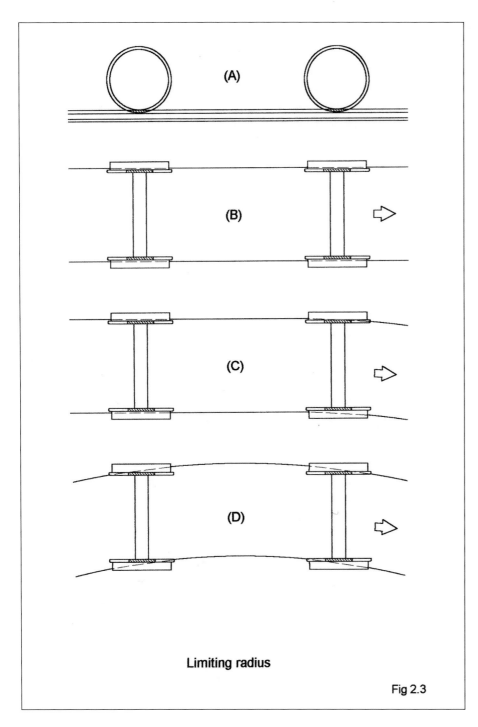

Limiting radius

Fig 2.3

distance between running faces of the rails. This cannot be taken too far, however, as if the gauge is too wide, short wheelbase vehicles will simply drop into the gap between the running faces.

Avoiding Kinks

On plain track, it is essential that we avoid any 'kinks' in the track, since these will frequently cause derailments as one or other flange meets and climbs over the rail head immediately after the kink.

At any one moment, the motion of a vehicle on a curve will be at a right angle to the line joining it to the centre of the curve. The line joining a point on a curve to its centre is called the *radius,* and, if you recall your school mathematics, a line touching a curve at right angles to the radius is called the *tangent.* The action of coning and/or flanges will ensure that when the vehicle is moving around a curve of constant radius its instantaneous direction of motion is always along the tangent.

Problems may occur, however, when the track changes from one curve to another. At the point where the curves meet, it is essential that there is no instantaneous change in direction. This means that the vehicle has to be travelling tangentially to *both* curves at the moment of transition. This can only be achieved if one simple condition is met: the centre points of the two curves and the point of transition must lie on the same straight line.

Referring to figure 2.4, case (1), you will see that the point of transition, marked 'X', lies on the straight line joining the centres of the two arcs, A and B. Thus at 'X', it is possible for the vehicle's motion to be tangential to both curves at the same time, as we require. In case (2), however, the two arc centres are not in a line with 'X' and there is consequently a decided kink in the track at this point.

To some extent, any errors in alignment will be taken up by the natural springiness of the rail itself. However,

calculator therefore gives you an option to set a tolerance on these dimensions.

For example, in theory an '0' gauge wagon with 21mm wheels and a 70mm wheelbase will derail on perfect track at a radius of around 10 inches. If the tolerance is set at 1%, however, this increases dramatically to almost three

feet. How many of us can guarantee that our wagons wheels run exactly true? A 1% error is only just over a quarter of a millimetre at this scale. In the smaller scales, it is correspondingly less.

The ability of vehicles to negotiate curves can be increased to some extent by gauge widening, that is increasing the

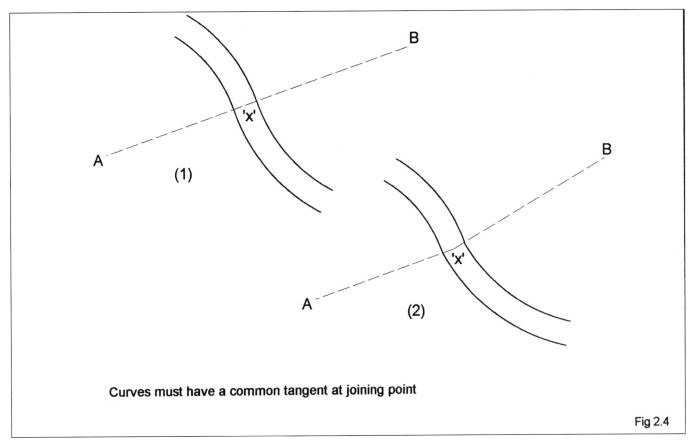

Curves must have a common tangent at joining point

Fig 2.4

the problem comes when separate lengths of rail have to be joined on curves, or when plain track joins up to points. There can be problems here even when the curve radius and centre do not change. Rail for track builders is generally sold in lengths of one metre. If one length of track is insufficient to cover a complete curve, then a join will have to be made on the curve, and here the spring of the rail will tend to take it back to its natural straight line. Thus at the ends of the length there will be a tendency for the radius to open out, and a similar situation to figure 2.4 (2) will result.

To avoid this, try to make joints on the straight, rather than around curves. If joints on curves are inevitable, then try to stagger them, i.e. make the joint in one rail a few centimetres before the joint in the other.

Points and Crossings

Despite all that has been said above, the potential pitfalls in plain track are as nothing compared with those

associated with points and crossings. These are generally the location of virtually all the 'trouble spots' on a model railway. Again a large part of avoiding difficulties here is down to geometry.

In figure 2.5 we show a representative point and identify its main components. Starting at what is known as the 'toe' end, a vehicle entering the point from the left will run initially along the two *stock rails*. Such a vehicle is running into the point in what is called the *facing* direction. A vehicle entering at the other end, known as the 'heel' end, would be entering the point in the *trailing* direction.

The vehicle entering in the facing direction encounters two separate parts of the point. First of all, it passes through the *switch* part, then over the *crossing*. We shall consider these two separately.

Switches

The function of the switch, as its name suggests, is to switch the vehicle entering the point in the facing direction

to one exit or the other at the heel end (a vehicle entering in the trailing direction does not have this choice available, although obviously the switch must be set the right way for it to exit at the toe end). The switching is actually carried out by two *switch rails*, which are specially planed to a taper. The switch rails may be either jointed at their heel end so that they are free to pivot, or they may be firmly fixed to the sleepers at their heel end and the natural flexibility of the metal may be used to achieve the switching action.

As shown in figure 2.5, the switch is set so that a vehicle entering the toe will be directed to the left hand, or diverging, exit. The switch rails may be moved by means of a *tie bar*, to direct the vehicle to the right hand, or straight ahead, exit. As drawn, however, the wheel flange of the left-hand wheel will pass between the left hand stock and switch rails, whereas the right hand wheel tread will roll smoothly from stock rail onto switch rail. To ensure that this

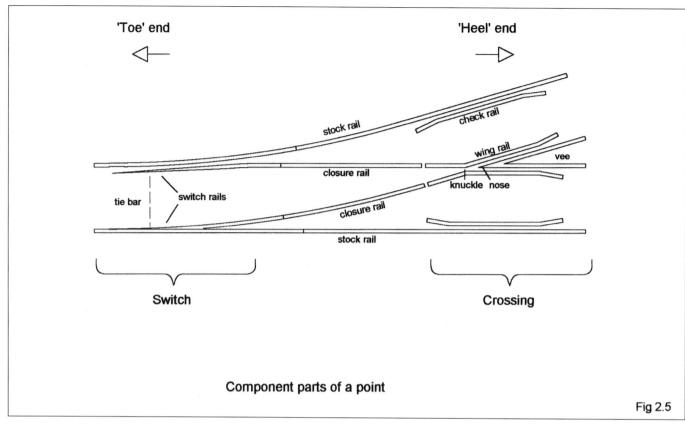

Component parts of a point

Fig 2.5

happens without problems, a number of factors must be just right.

Referring to figure 2.6, we see the situation at the instant the wheels enter the toe end of the switch. The enlarged insets show how the stock rail is held in a special *slide chair,* which allows, as its name suggests, the switch rails to slide left and right. On the left side the switch rail is in the open position. Notice that the opening is sufficiently wide to ensure that the wheel flange clears the switch rail completely, even if the opposite flange is touching the rail on that side. It is essential that this opening is sufficiently wide to prevent the flange getting inside the switch rail under any circumstances.

On the right hand side, the switch rail is hard up against the stock rail. To achieve this, the stock rail will either be filed away slightly to allow the tapered end of the switch rail to be housed in a slight recess, or it will be bent outwards slightly for a short distance. The latter practice, known as *joggling,* was prevalent on the Great Western, most

other railway companies preferring the former method. The key here is that there must be no gap between the switch and stock rails which might allow the flange to get between them.

The consequence of either of these two essential conditions not being met may well be that one pair of wheels of a vehicle goes one way over the switch, and the second pair goes the other way. The vehicle will continue crab-wise for a short distance, then it will cause a spectacular derailment, not only of itself, but possibly of the entire train! Note that any obstructions in the switch, such as dirt, loose ballast, etc. will also prevent its correct operation.

On the prototype, switches in which the switch rails were free to pivot were referred to by length, e.g. as 10 foot switches, 12 foot switches, etc. The later flexible switches were referred to by letters A, B, C, etc. Type A switches were the shortest, and on the prototype they went up to type G which were 60 feet long. Modellers rarely go above the 30 foot type D switches, however.

Crossings

At the opposite end of the point, we have the crossing. Actually, to give it its full title, it is an acute crossing. There is another sort that we shall meet later. Unlike the switch, this has no moving parts so to some extent it may be thought that it would provide fewer problems. However, it can still be a source of several pitfalls as we shall see.

Between the switch and the crossing, the vehicle will move along one or other of the two pairs of stock rails and *closure* rails. A glance at figure 2.5 will reveal that, as the right hand wheel approaches the straight stock rail, we could be heading for a problem. The wheel flange, with the point as shown, will eventually need to pass through the straight closure rail, which it obviously cannot do. We therefore need a gap in this rail, which is known as the *knuckle.* A similar gap would be required for the flange of the left hand wheel to pass the curved closure rail if the point were set the other way.

After the knuckle, the wheels will

encounter the *vee* of the crossing. Here, they will rejoin the rails with their flanges, hopefully, on the correct side. However, because there is a gap between the knuckle and the nose of the vee, this is not ensured. The wheel flange would be free to move laterally at this gap, and might well hit the nose of the vee or even pass to the wrong side of it.

To eliminate this possibility, we introduce on the stock rail side of the crossing a pair of *check rails.* Referring to figure 2.7, we see that the function of the check rail is to ensure that, were there to be any lateral movement to the right (and the wheel coning for one thing would tend to cause this), then the inside of the flange on the left hand wheel makes contact with the check rail before there is any possibility of the right hand wheel flange getting the wrong side of the nose of the vee.

Obviously, the dimensions and spacing of these components are very important. The size of the gap between the check rail and the stock rail is referred to as the *flangeway,* and its value is critical. Too large a flangeway gap will fail to prevent the flange hitting the crossing nose. Too small a gap will cause the flange to foul the *wing rails* (see figure 2.5). Another important consideration is the width of the tread on the wheels. If this is too narrow, the wheel will drop into the gap at the knuckle and ride up again over the crossing nose. At best, this will give rise to unsightly bouncing of vehicles on crossings. At worst, it will be another source of derailments.

Crossing Vee Angles

We come now to another issue of geometry. The angle made by the vee of a crossing is its most important dimension and on the prototype this was described in terms of a ratio between two lengths. In essence, these were the ratio of a distance *along* the vee, and the distance *between* the running faces. Thus a crossing with a very large angle might be described as 1 in 3, meaning that three feet from the nose, the running faces were one foot apart. A more

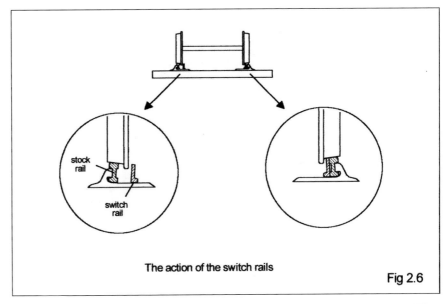

The action of the switch rails

Fig 2.6

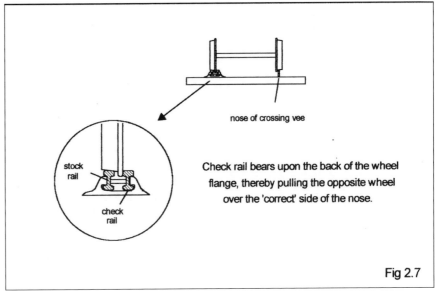

nose of crossing vee

Check rail bears upon the back of the wheel flange, thereby pulling the opposite wheel over the 'correct' side of the nose.

Fig 2.7

shallow angle might be 1 in 6, and so on. Note that 1 in 6 is often written 1:6.

There has been much debate and discussion about the details of how these lengths were measured. There are basically three different schemes, illustrated in figure 2.8. All of them yield very slightly different angles for a given ratio. We shall not enter the debate about which of them is the 'correct' method, but we shall dismiss them all by saying, possibly somewhat controversially, that they are *all wrong!*

A glance at the final diagram in figure

2.8 should convince the reader that there is no way of getting two 1 in 4 angles to add up to the same as a 1 in 2 angle by any of these methods. It is quite simply impossible to draw two 1:4 triangles such that the sum of their two angles, A, is the same as angle B in the 1:2 triangle. The centre line measure (the most commonly used), gives a 1:4 angle as 14.25°. The sum of two of these is 28.50°. However, by centre line measure, 28.50° is not 1:2, it is 1:1.96875. A 1:2 angle, by centre line measure, is actually 28.075°, almost half a degree less.

The only way of getting accurate

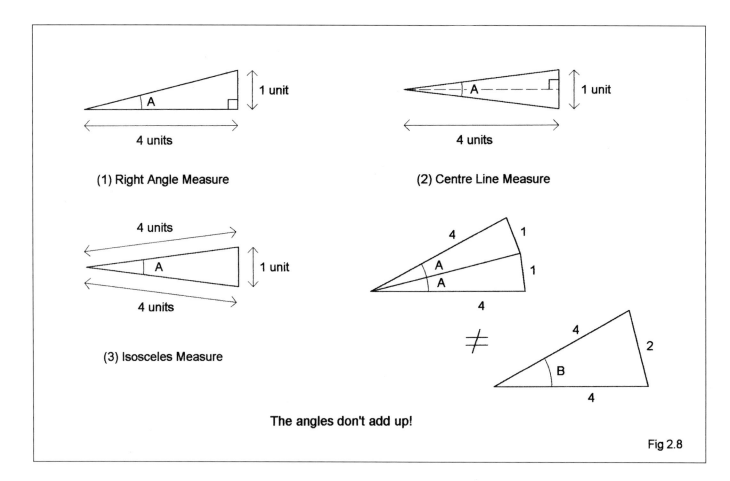

(1) Right Angle Measure

(2) Centre Line Measure

(3) Isosceles Measure

The angles don't add up!

Fig 2.8

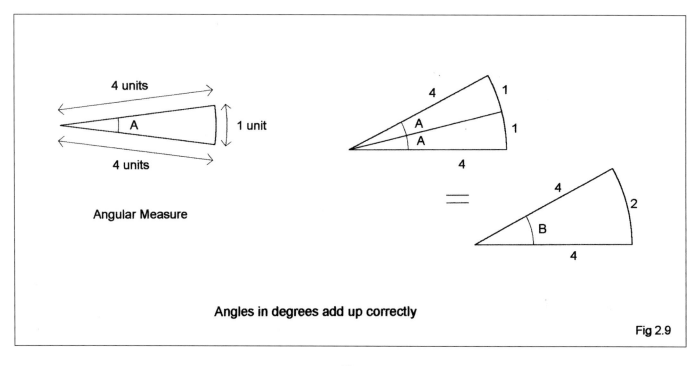

Angular Measure

Angles in degrees add up correctly

Fig 2.9

angles is to use *angular measure,* as illustrated in figure 2.9. This measures the distance between running faces not along a straight line, but around an *arc* with its centre at the intersection point of the crossing nose.

You might well ask why, if this is the only accurate method of measuring angles, did the railway builders use '1 in N' type measures? The answer is twofold. Firstly, the difference is only slight, and would be easily taken up by slight misalignment of track and/or bending of the rails. Secondly, the measurement of a distance around an arc would be extremely difficult out in the field. Straight line measures required only a piece of string and chalk. Angular measure would require much more complicated equipment.

You might then ask, if it was good enough for the prototype, should it not be good enough for us? The answer, in the author's view, is no. Referring to figure 2.10, you will see illustrated the central

part of a scissors crossing. If the two main lines are to be parallel, then the angle B must be exactly twice angle A. As we have seen, this is not achieved if angles A are 1:4 and B is 1:2.

The *Trax* program, therefore, works internally entirely in angular measure. Although you can specify points as 1:6, 1:8 etc, these are immediately converted to degrees, and all subsequent calculations by *Trax* are done in these units.

Curved Vees

On early prototypes, the crossing of a point would utilise a vee with straight edges. All of the necessary curvature for the point would be taken up in the switch rails, which would have a curvature dependent on their length, and the closure rails, which would often be bent on-site to join up with the crossing vee at the appropriate location. Tables would be available to give the correct distance from the switch rail ends to the crossing nose. This distance was referred to as the

lead of the point. Through the crossing itself, all of the rails would be straight.

This makes for simpler construction, of course, and most ready-built points for model railways are of this type. In models, it also proves useful in helping to prevent buffer locking when the curved ends of two points are joined together. Instead of having a reverse curve, similar to that illustrated in figure 2.4 (1), on which long bogie coaches are prone to getting their buffers interlocked, you would have a straight section between the curves.

Depending on your tastes, however, you might prefer the appearance of a point in which the curve is taken right on through the crossing vee itself. For the same turnout angle, such a point would have a considerably larger radius than one with a straight vee, as illustrated by figure 2.11. We have seen that larger radii tend to mean better running, for various reasons, and there are other ways of overcoming the buffer locking

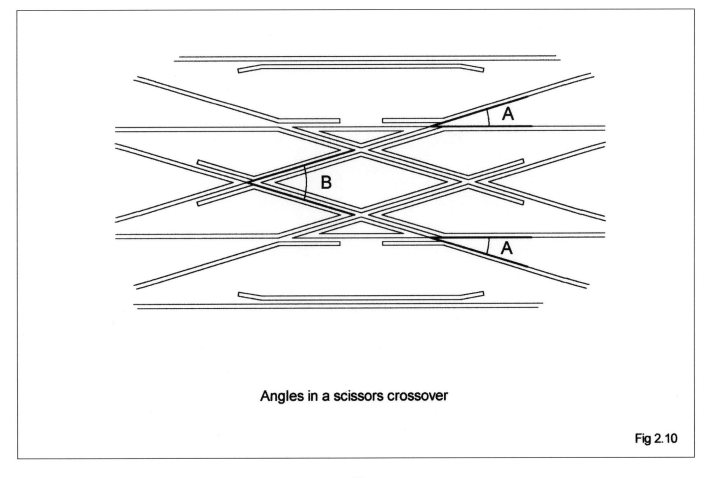

Angles in a scissors crossover

Fig 2.10

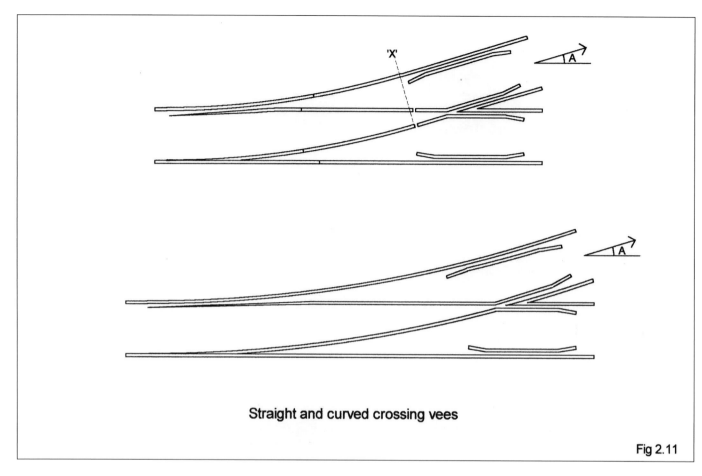

Straight and curved crossing vees

Fig 2.11

problem. It is entirely a matter of personal preference.

One case, however, where curved vees are generally used is on curved points, i.e. those in which both stock rails are curved to different radii, and/or directions. Curved points with straight vees just don't look good at all in the opinion of the authors. The *Trax* program will allow you to specify standard points with either straight or curved vees when printing your templates. Curved points are always drawn with curved vees. The straight point with a curved vee is, in fact, a special case of the latter, where the radius of one curve is taken out to infinity.

Obtuse Crossings

As was said earlier, the type of crossing we get in a point is called an acute crossing. This is because the angle made by the two running faces is less than 90°, i.e. it is an acute angle. If an angle is greater than 90° we call it obtuse. In a diamond crossing (see figure 2.12), this is what we require at the centre of the diamond. The figure illustrates the component parts of an obtuse crossing, the elbow rail, point rails and the elbow check rail.

From figure 2.12, it is clear that the two 'gaps' in the opposite sides of the obtuse crossing overlap to some extent. This can be a source of problems, as the elbow check rail cannot fulfil its function across the whole length of the gap. In figure 2.13, we demonstrate the danger. On the left, we see a pair of wheels correctly negotiating a well-laid crossing. However, on the right, the point rail at 'x' has been laid a little out of line. The track gauge at this point is a little too narrow, and as a result the wheel flange is going to strike the end of the point rail. Because there is a gap on the opposite side, the flange has a 50-50 chance whether it rolls to the left or right

of point 'x'. The wheel pair could thus take the 'wrong' exit and cause a major derailment.

The problem gets worse as the crossing angle becomes shallower, and for this reason crossing angles smaller than 1 in 8 are rarely used.

The Importance of Track Gauges

From what has been said, it is clear that the essential consideration is accuracy of measurement. The gauge between running faces, the width of flangeways and the accuracy both of the wheel profile and its fitting to the axle, are all of great importance.

To ensure that your track conforms to the necessary criteria you should obtain at an absolute minimum two accurate track gauges, as illustrated in figure 2.14. These will be used during construction to hold running rails, check rails and other components in position so as to keep the key dimensions accurate.

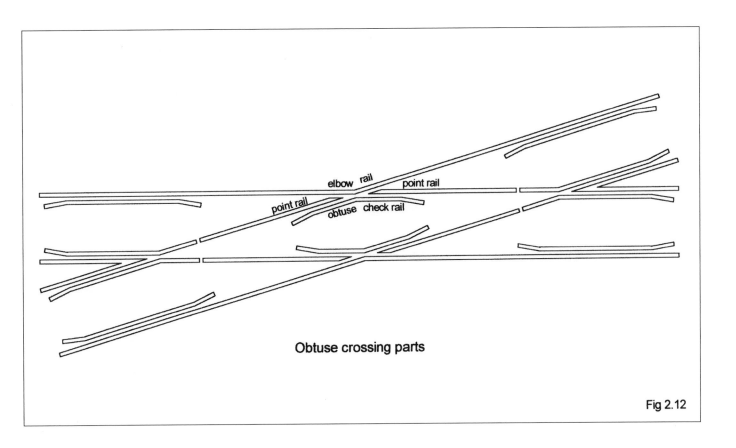

Obtuse crossing parts

Fig 2.12

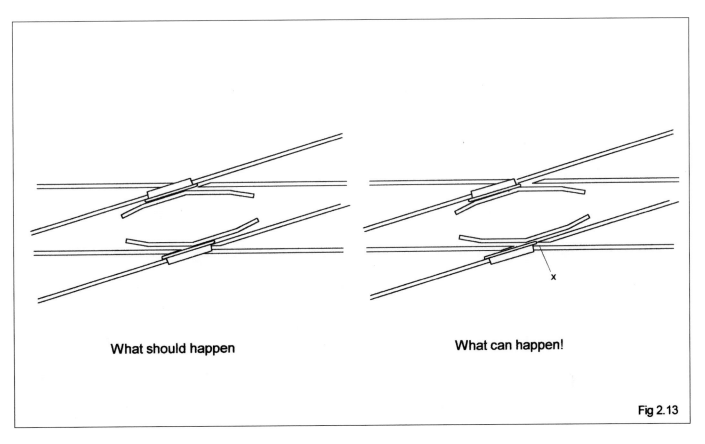

What should happen

What can happen!

x

Fig 2.13

These dimensions are highlighted in figure 2.15. They are the *track gauge,* G, the *flangeway,* FW, the *back-to-back* wheel measurement, BB, the flange *thickness,* FT, and the *over flanges* measurement, OF.

Table 2.1 gives some typical values of these measurements for a variety of scales, gauges and standards. The *Trax* program, however, will let you enter any reasonable values for these so that you can build trackwork to your own standards.

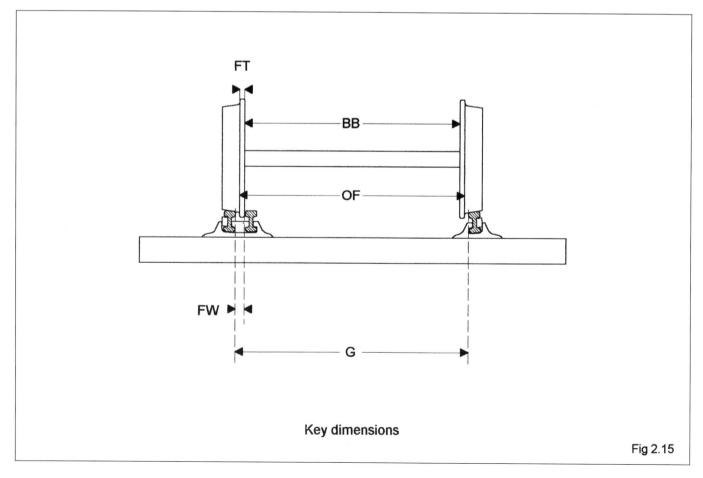

Key dimensions

Fig 2.15

TABLE 2.1

Gauge & Standard	Scale 1 ft =	G mm	BB mm	FW mm	FT mm	OF mm	Between Tracks
Gauge 1	10 mm	45	40	2.50	2.0	44	115
O fine	7 mm	32	29	1.75	0.75-1.0	30.5	80
O course	7 mm	32	28	2.20	0.75-1.5	30.25	80
O USA	1/4 in	32	29	2.00	1.0	31.0	80
ScaleSeven	7 mm	33	31.20-31.30	1.00	0.63	29.94	77.5
OO	4 mm	16.5	14.7	1.00	0.65	16.0	45
EM	4 mm	18.2	16.5	1.00	0.65	17.8	45
P4	4 mm	18.83	17.67-17.75	0.68	0.35-0.4	18.46	45
HO	3.5 mm	16.5	14.7	1.00	0.65	16.0	45
3 mm	3 mm	14.2	12.5	0.75	0.65	13.8	35
N	2 mm	9	8	0.50	0.3	8.6	25

And you thought you had alignment problems. This is the prototype at Waterloo in 1936, relaying and maintaining the service! Sadly it seems impossible for our modern railway network to undertake both these actions simultaneously today.

Fig. 3.1   Standard pattern of sleeper spacing at rail joints

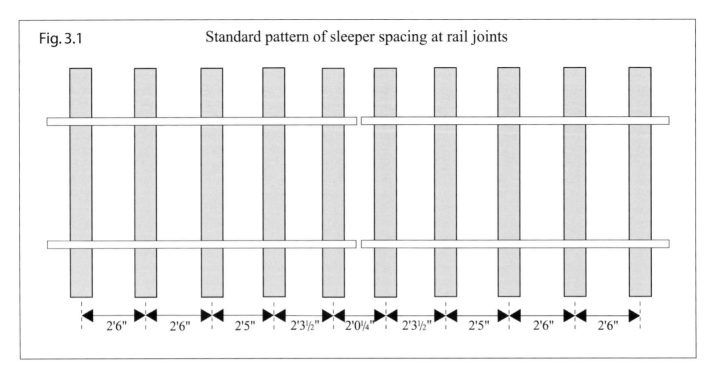

Mixed bull-head and flat-bottom track on the same running line? Well not quite as in this case the camera has deceived the eye. What is actually being seen is a bull-head check-rail, and necessary because of the sharp curve on the approach to Paddington. Flat-bottom rail has too wide a foot to be used as a check-rail unless the foot is machined narrower.

ELEMENTS OF TRACK CONSTRUCTION

Construction and Laying of Plain Track

Preparation of a suitable base

Baseboard construction does not feature in this book, so it is assumed that a suitable firm, flat base is available for the track work. It has been the normal practice for many years to add a sub base of sheet cork or other rubber based material to help reduce noise and also to give the impression that the ballast is deeper than it really is. The material is usually chamfered at the edge to represent the shoulder of the ballast when stuck down.

If building a layout where the baseboards will be dismantled from time to time, consideration must be given to the fixing of sleepers at the baseboard joins. A simple solution is to use a copper clad sleeper screwed down and have the rails soldered to it or soldered to brass chairs that are in turn soldered in position.

If using the more spongy rubber base, replace with a suitable thickness of wood to firmly support the last sleeper. Wherever possible pre-prepare the track passing over a join and lay the length of track across without cutting the rails. Solder or fix the sleepers down at the join and when all is dry and firm, cut the rails carefully to divide the track. This method also applies to any point work that needs to bridge a baseboard join. It may be necessary to move a sleeper or even lay it at an angle, but this should be avoided if possible as it will spoil the look of the finished track. It is better to cut through a sleeper even at a strange angle using a fine saw. Whenever possible position rail ends to coincide with a baseboard join and having cut the rail, add half a cosmetic fishplate to each rail. In this way the sleeper spacing, being closer, will add strength to the rail ends.

Laying ready-made track

The use of ready-made track can speed up the track laying process. However, it is all too easy to bodge the job and regret the hasty efforts made. The prototype until recent times laid track in various lengths, some 30 feet, some 45 feet and the later normal length was 60 feet. The sleeper spacing for the majority of the sleepers was a 2' 6" centre. At the ends of each length of rail the sleeper spacing was amended as fig 3.1 opposite shows.

The wooden keys inserted in the chairs to hold the rail to gauge were hammered in to certain rules. This ensured that the motion of the train, particularly the locomotive drive wheels,

A fine example of EM track-work built using rail soldered to copper-clad sleepers.

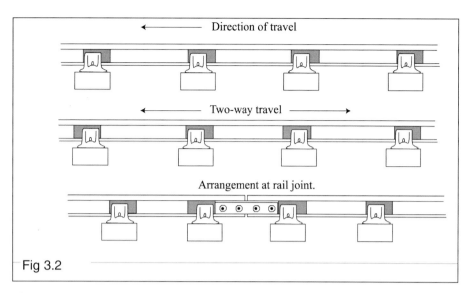

Fig 3.2

Direction of travel

Two-way travel

Arrangement at rail joint.

were encouraging the key into the gap and not allowing it to become loose. Regular checks were made by staff to knock any loose keys back into place. At the joining of two rail lengths, the keys were knocked in so that room was left for the fishplates to be positioned between the two adjoining sleepers. The drawing above shows this clearly.

As we start in the model railway hobby we usually take steps to purchase ready built track in yard or metre lengths and join the ends with metal slide-on fishplates without amending any sleeper spacing.

If you are intending to go to the trouble of building your point work, it will pay to spend a little time adapting the ready-made track that is available to represent more accurately the prototype. Sleeper spacing can easily be amended at the ends of each length of purchased track. Use a simple jig to close the spacing and trim the rails to give the correct space after the last sleeper.

Provided the layout is not in the garden where extremes of temperature exist, the yard or metre length can remain in one piece, but measure where the 60 ft join would be and, by cutting the web between the sleepers, move them to the correct spacing. Cut part way through the rail and add cosmetic fishplates. In the smaller gauges you will get more than two 60 ft lengths from a full-length piece

Note the facility on this jig to use two 12" sleepers laid where the cosmetic rail joints will be.

This O gauge track jig allows four lengths of track to be constructed at one filling. The owner of the jig constructed most of his track whilst recovering from a hip replacement - that's forward thinking.

of track so, do the same for each 60 ft length finally cutting the track to match the nearest 60 ft prototype end.

In O gauge a purchased length can represent only two lengths and you will cut away a small amount. (An alternative in O gauge would be to divide the full length in two halves and amend the sleeper spacing there. By moving up the remaining sleepers to their correct spacing, only a small amount of rail needs to be lost at the end.)

A well known O gauge layout, that sadly no longer exists, used to run a set of Pullman coaches around a continuous circuit and using the front pair of wheels on each coach as a measure, 'V's were filed into the rails to represent the rail joints. As a result, pairs of wheels on every coach struck the cosmetic track joins at the same time. The clicketty-click from the rail joints was very impressive and was a feature remembered from that visit.

Plastic cosmetic fishplates are available in all the popular scales and some of them are designed to hold the rail firmly in line, at least whilst the track is being fixed to the base. These also have a spacing piece that stops the two rails joining and giving an electrical short where there should be an electrical break.

Building Track

All the above information regarding sleeper spacing, key direction and track laying generally applies to this section also. The extra ingredient when building track from scratch is the use of track gauges. Some of the finer tolerance scale/gauge relationships, e.g. EM produce their own special track gauges that automatically widen the gauge very slightly when constructing curved track. The clearances within locomotives allowing for any side-play and track tolerances are much finer in EM, P4 and Scale 7. The gauge needs to be widened when laying to the usual 'model' sharp curves. In OO and Fine-scale 7mm, there is sufficient side-play built within the stock to enable the same track gauge to be used throughout the layout.

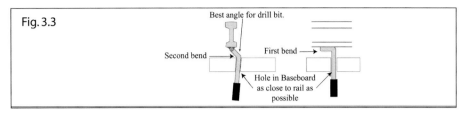

Fig. 3.3
Best angle for drill bit.
Second bend
First bend
Hole in Baseboard as close to rail as possible

If building many lengths of track a jig is beneficial and will save time in the long run. See the photograph of a typical O gauge jig allowing 4 lengths to be made at one session. The jig allows sleepers to be spaced correctly. If laying straight track, both rails are fixed to the sleepers at the same time. With curved track it is recommended that only one rail is fixed to the sleepers, the formation removed from the jig and the inner curved rail fitted in situ over the track plan using the track gauges. Cosmetic rail joints will be cut or filed into the top half of the rail when laid and fishplates added.

Wiring Track

Many layouts are spoilt by the visible signs of wiring. In the perfect world, having a template for the track, you could pre-drill holes to allow the wire to come through the baseboard directly under the rails. We do not live in a perfect world, and although you will know where all your track feeds need to be from the *Trax* drawing of your layout, wiring is something that takes a back seat when concentrating on the track building and laying.

A tip. Having laid today's section of track, go back and solder the wire droppers to yesterdays track that was laid. Do this because the rail will still be clean and will take the solder more easily.

- Drill a hole as close to the rail as possible.
- Cut a length of wire long enough to reach your tag strip underneath, remembering it may need to pass through holes in timber underneath.
- Strip off at least 12mm, twist the wire cores together and tin the wire with solder.

- Make two 90° bends as shown in fig 3.3.
- Add flux to the tinned end. (This will transfer to the rail and saves adding flux there.)
- Push the other end through the baseboard and position your tinned end with flux UNDER the rail.
- Heat the contact position with an iron and you will have a reliable electrical connection UNDER the rail that will be hidden by the ballast at a later date.

The layout of 'Coventry' (see photograph on next page) has used this method. When, on the rare occasion, a fault occurs it is very hard to see the wires and it needs a search under the boards to locate them.

Every length of rail should have an electrical feed. DO NOT RELY ON METAL FISHPLATES FOR ELECTRICAL CONNECTIONS.

Fixing the Completed Track and Point Work to the Baseboard.

The more common way to fix the track down is by using white PVA glue, spreading thinly along the route and laying the track down into the glue. After careful alignment the track should be weighted whilst the glue dries.

An alternative method when using plastic sleepers, is to use the same plastic solvent to stick the sleepers to the cork. Dry laying can continue until all associated track is joined to point work, etc, and when alignment is correct, place the solvent around some of the sleepers. At baseboard ends, screw the sleepers down as previously described.

Future ballasting will fix the track firmly. Ballasting with granite chips is better laid dry and when satisfied with the results, add a mixture of white PVA

Coventry track work. A curved diamond crossing and point. Part of the complex point work at the 'up' end of Coventry Station that leads to Coventry Loco Shed and Leamington. 7mm.

glue and water with a little washing up liquid to help the glue spread.

Point Construction

The following guide is designed for the modeller who wishes to produce good looking and reliable track-work. All layouts have points on them and therefore they form an essential part of the track-work. A poorly built or laid point will cause chaos at any running session so great care is needed in following a few simple rules. You will by now have designed your layout and made decisions about the standards you wish to use. You will have set a minimum radius for curves. This must also apply to points. You will have decided what code of rail to use, (the code given to rail is the height of the rail expressed as thousands of an inch, e.g. code 75 rail is 75 thou' of an inch high or 0.075"). You will also have chosen whether your sleepers are copper-clad, wood or plastic.

With the above in mind we can build our first point using the plan printed off on your computer from the *Trax* program.

The basic requirements for all track and point construction are:

1. A flat surface to work on.
2. A straight edge.
3. Track gauges.
4. An accurate plan or a copy of the plan. (Care, photocopying any drawing tends to enlarge it slightly each time. The plan in this case can only be used as a guide.)
5. Simple tools including a soldering iron.
6. Some method of fixing sleepers to the plan and the plan to the work surface. We recommend 'display mount' as used by photographers that provides a light fix. This is essential if we are not to damage the point when removing it from the plan as some sleepers have only slide chairs holding the rail to the sleepers.
7. The raw materials you intend to use.
8. The most important tool, your eyes. Smooth flowing curves or straight track are best laid with a good eye.

The following guide is based on a construction of plastic sleepers and plastic chairs. If using copper-clad sleepers and either no chairs or cosmetic chairs you will need to adapt the guidance notes accordingly.

Notes About the Following Construction Details.

The *Trax* program only shows sleepers that start at the blade and finish at the place where, if two like points were joined together they would form a crossover. If building a 'stand alone' point extend the toe of the point by at least 2 sleepers and do not trim the vee or stock rails at the other end until joining to other track work. The following drawings have the additional sleepers added.

If building a complex of points the order of construction may need amending. The important consideration is track alignment so that when looking along the completed track work, it flows smoothly without kinks.

The notes are based on those issued by "C & L Finescale". The method described is best suited for plastic sleepers and plastic chairs using a plastic solvent for fixing. This applies to all scales and gauges although we have suggested the use of copper clad strips or copper clad sleepers for strength and electrical bonding.

After building a standard point you will soon adapt your own techniques to cover all the possible variables.

Stages to Building a Point

Fig 3.4 gives the usual names given to point work parts.

Stage 1 - Fig 3.5

Fix the *Trax* plan to a flat surface; such as a piece of 12mm MDF using the display mount type glue.

Prepare sleepers from the material you intend to use, cutting to length as necessary.

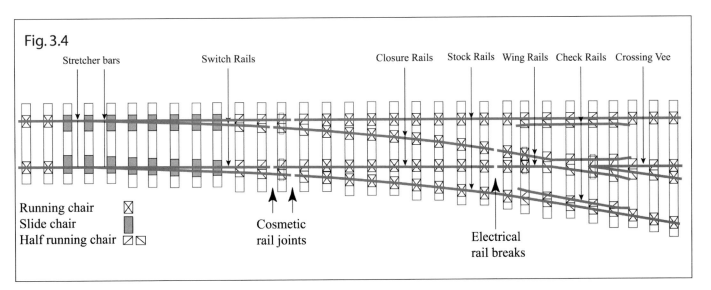

Fig. 3.4

Stretcher bars   Switch Rails   Closure Rails   Stock Rails   Wing Rails   Check Rails   Crossing Vee

Running chair ⊠
Slide chair ▣
Half running chair ◩◪

Cosmetic rail joints

Electrical rail breaks

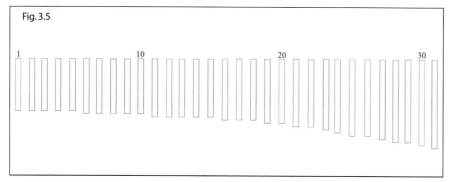

Fig. 3.5

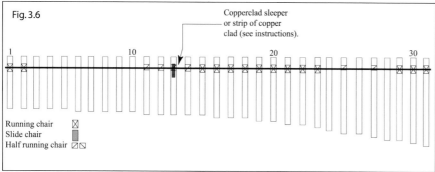

Fig. 3.6

Copperclad sleeper
or strip of copper
clad (see instructions).

Running chair ⊠
Slide chair ▮
Half running chair ⊠◺

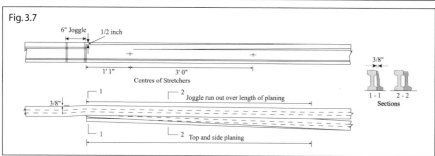

Fig. 3.7

6" Joggle   1/2 inch

1' 1"   3' 0"
Centres of Stretchers

3/8"

1 - 1   2 - 2
Sections

Joggle run out over length of planing

Top and side planing

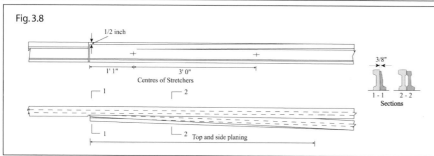

Fig. 3.8

1/2 inch

1' 1"   3' 0"
Centres of Stretchers

3/8"

1 - 1   2 - 2
Sections

Top and side planing

Mask with scraps of paper the area outside the sleepers and spray the top surface of the plan with display mount.

Using a straight edge (if the point is to have one straight track), place the sleepers onto the plan in the marked positions.

Stage 2 - Figs 3.6 to 3.8

It is normal practice to put a joggle into the stock rails to accommodate the point blades. This can be done by bending the rail or filing away part of the rail. In any event the amount of diversion is small but sufficient to allow the blade to fit snugly into the recess and give a smooth passage for any wheel to pass over. See fig 3.7 for details of a 'joggled' stock rail and fig 3.8 for the more usual modellers equivalent where the stock rail remains straight but has the inner face filed away.

Electrical bonding is required to connect the stock rail to the closure rails and also to connect the vee with the wing rails. One method is to use a copper clad sleeper of the same thickness in place of a plastic one. Brass chairs are available so that the rail can be soldered to the chair that is, in turn, soldered to the sleeper. (The sleeper will need a gap cut in the copper clad to prevent an electrical short between the running rails.) Another method in O gauge is to superglue a small piece of 1mm thick copper clad to the plastic sleeper as shown on the drawings. The copper clad need only extend to the outside of each rail and will later be hidden by cosmetic chairs.

File off any burrs from the rail end and taper the web and base to allow the plastic chairs to slide on without damage.

Slide chairs as required onto the first stock rail (the straightest), remembering the direction of keys if modelled on the chairs. Leave a gap where slide chairs are to be positioned and note that where checkrails are to be fitted, leave gaps as shown. Also omit the chair where the copper clad strip is shown (or use a brass chair for a copper clad sleeper).

Fix the first and last chairs to the appropriate sleepers using the plan remembering that the *Trax* plans show the running face of rails. If the point is a straight point look along the rail to ensure it is straight. Ensure the joggle or recessed face is in the right position.

Now fix a chair near the centre of the point and make the same checks.

Continue to fix the running chairs to the sleepers checking continually.

Stage 3 - Fig 3.9 to 3.11

The 'frog' or crossing vee is fitted next. See figs 3.10 and 3.11 for the correct way to prepare such a vee if you intend to build your own. The top planing need only be 2 or 3 light strokes with a file. Also note that the vee is not finished to a sharp point. Again use a file to blunt the point slightly. If the vee is to have curved rails, introduce the curves before soldering the two parts together.

Check its position on the plan and you will see that the nose of the frog is always over a sleeper. You will note that the crossing vee (in the example) has two straight rails, which will mean that your point will have a straight section for the two diverging routes. In model terms this is recommended and avoids buffer locking if the next curve were to be in the opposite direction. This is all down to personal preference. Examine the track on the prototype you are copying. If the crossing rails at the vee are curved then introduce the curve now. Remember also the 1 in 20 cant of the rails. Are you going to introduce this at the vee? If not the next few plastic chairs will struggle to push the rail into this cant. If making your own vee, introduce this cant in each rail when preparing using some plastic chairs to hold the rails at the correct angle.

Slide a chair on each rail. Other chairs will be fitted later. Using two track gauges, position the frog and solder to the copper clad. (Care not to unsolder the vee.) Now fix the 2 chairs to the final sleeper.

Stage 4 - Fig 3.12

Take the curved stock rail. Position it roughly in place to determine the position of the joggle and bend or file appropriately. It is normal to start the curvature of the stock rail with a bend at the joggle. This bend matches the blade shape and allows the straight blade to fit correctly (see fig 3.12). Add the appropriate chairs to the rail remembering to leave gaps as before.

Using two gauges at the toe of the point fix the chairs for the short straight piece ensuring the joggles are opposite each other.

Remove the track gauges and position them at the vee end and curve the rail so that it follows the plan. If you previously curved your crossing rail, ensure the track gauges reproduce that curve at the end of the stock rail.

Fix the chairs in position checking by eye that a smooth curve is adopted

Above: An example of a point modelled with joggled stock rails - yes it is a model!

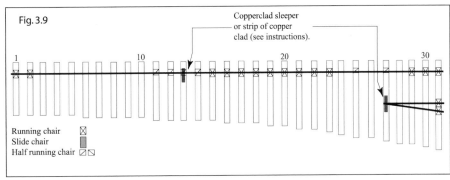

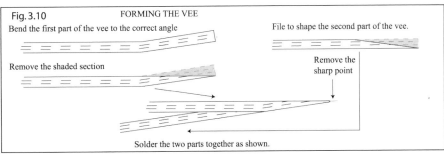

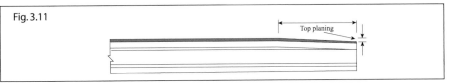

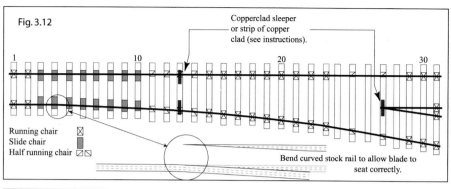

Fig. 3.12

Copperclad sleeper or strip of copper clad (see instructions).

Running chair
Slide chair
Half running chair

Bend curved stock rail to allow blade to seat correctly.

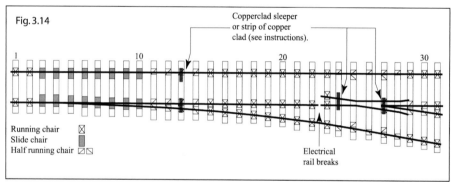

Fig. 3.13

Copperclad sleeper or strip of copper clad (see instructions).

Running chair
Slide chair
Half running chair

Electrical rail breaks

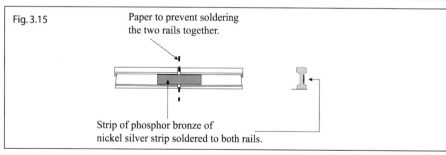

Fig. 3.14

Copperclad sleeper or strip of copper clad (see instructions).

Running chair
Slide chair
Half running chair

Electrical rail breaks

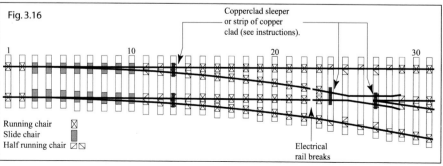

Fig. 3.15

Paper to prevent soldering the two rails together.

Strip of phosphor bronze of nickel silver strip soldered to both rails.

Fig. 3.16

Copperclad sleeper or strip of copper clad (see instructions).

Running chair
Slide chair
Half running chair

Electrical rail breaks

and add the slide chairs to both stock rails.

Stage 5 - Fig 3.13

Prepare the wing rails. The length can be copied from the track plan unless a baseboard join dictates differently. On the drawing the electrical gap, which can also be a baseboard join, can be anywhere between sleeper 14 and sleeper 24. To achieve a crisp bend at the knuckle, cut through the rail on the inside of the bend with a piercing saw or fine rail saw. If laying the track at the correct cant the cut will need to be at an angle or one part of the wing rail will point skywards.

Lay the wing rail for the straight track first using at least two gauges to give the track gauge and correct flange width.

Stage 6 - Figs 3.14 and 3.15

Prepare and lay the second wing rail ensuring that the knuckles are opposite each other. Trim to length so that the electrical gap is central between two sleepers.

Add the remaining half chairs to the vee and wing rails.

Now prepare and lay the straight closure rail and blade.

Look again at figs 3.7 and 3.8 - page 32, and note how the blade needs to have some top planning so that it will sit just below the stock rail. The chart on the next page gives the basic dimensions of common standard points (GWR) including the length of planning required.

With a file - re-shape the running face of the blade to a knife-edge. Check to see that it fits snugly into the joggle of the stock rail.

If laying the more modern sprung blade, the closure rail and blade will be in one piece. If using the shorter pivoted blades, the closure rail should be cut to length. Prepare the blade as above and using a small piece of phosphor bronze or nickel silver (acting as one half of a fishplate), solder the blade and closure rail together using a piece of paper or card between the rails to avoid solder running into the joint. Leave a gap

Type of Switch	Crossing Angle 1 in	Length of Planing
	6	
B	7	8' 4"
	8	
	8	
C	9	10' 5"
	10	
	10	
D	11	12' 4"
	12	
	13	

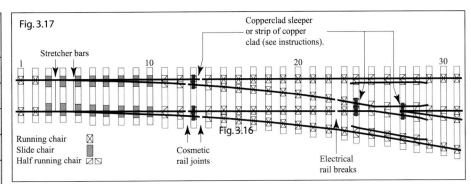

Below, A close-up photograph showing how stretcher bars are fitted to model points.

between the rails to represent the rail join and allow for the movement. See the drawing. The metal strip should be on the outer face of the rail. The inner running face needs a cosmetic fishplate to cover the join stuck only to one rail. Check the flexibility of the join and lay as if using sprung blades.

Add chairs and a plastic rail joiner if required before using the gauges once again to fix the rail to the sleepers.

Stage 7 - Fig 3.16

Repeat the above for the curved closure rail and blade.

Stage 8 - Fig 3.17 and 3.18

Form check rails using the plan for guidance on length. Note that the check rails should always end opposite the wing rail ends. They normally stretch over 5 sleepers and 3 chairs can now be added. Fix into position using gauges. Add the half chairs to both the checkrail and stock rail. Add the half chairs either side of the copper-clad strips amending as necessary to fit.

Add stretcher bars using the drawing as a guide. There are many ways to operate a point so bear this mind when designing a stretcher bar. The system shown has been used many times on several O gauge layouts, and allows flexibility in the movement and looks very much like the prototype from normal viewing distance. The use of the double sided copper-clad ensures that the metal stretcher bar is electrically isolated from both blades. By allowing the copper-clad to run under the stock rail, the blade is held down. Do not rely on the copper-clad to conduct track power to the blade. This must be achieved by wiring the blades to the stock rail or using the copper-clad strips already mentioned.

The use of a piece of paper during the soldering ensures no spread of solder to parts where it is not needed, and also gives a small tolerance or clearance between the moving parts.

Finally, make sure the electrical breaks are where you expect them to be and add cosmetic fishplates.

Before removing the point from the paper template, superglue the slide chairs to the rail, as they are not physically fixed to the rail by any other means. If you have used the spray-mount type method to fix the sleepers to the template, you should be able to peel off the paper having turned the point over. Any sleepers that refuse to let go can be repositioned and glued again.

Bond any rails together if the copper-clad was not used.

Add a touch of impact adhesive glue under the stretcher bars to prevent them dropping out when tipping up the layout at a later time.

Stretcher Bar Construction and Fitting

Fig. 3.18

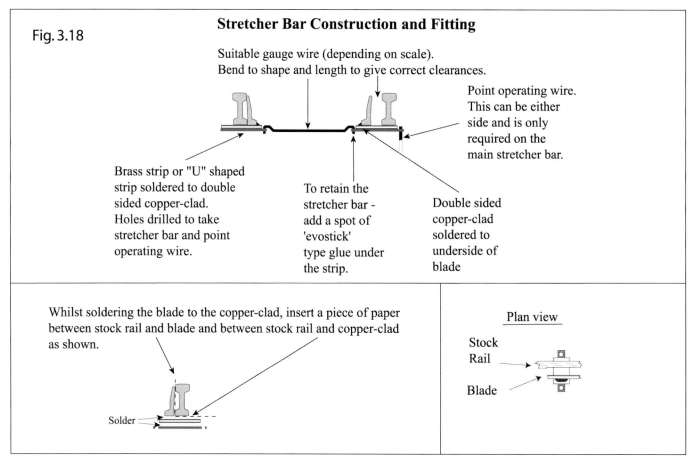

Suitable gauge wire (depending on scale).
Bend to shape and length to give correct clearances.

Point operating wire. This can be either side and is only required on the main stretcher bar.

Brass strip or "U" shaped strip soldered to double sided copper-clad. Holes drilled to take stretcher bar and point operating wire.

To retain the stretcher bar - add a spot of 'evostick' type glue under the strip.

Double sided copper-clad soldered to underside of blade

Whilst soldering the blade to the copper-clad, insert a piece of paper between stock rail and blade and between stock rail and copper-clad as shown.

Solder

Plan view

Stock Rail

Blade

Point Operation

The choice of method will be determined by several factors.

1. Is the layout portable and is the control of the points to pass over baseboard joins?
2. Is the layout to be operated from several positions?
3. Your engineering/DIY capabilities.
4. Is the layout to operated from a central position, e.g. a lever frame or control panel?
5. Is the layout to have electrical or or mechanical interlocking to prevent a conflicting move?

Many of us build layouts that are capable of being exhibited. If you are able to get both sides of the layout for building and operating purposes you will need to decide which side of the layout the public will view.

There are advantages in all methods of point operation. My personal preference is to use some form of electrical operation of the stretcher bars, operated by a lever within an interlocking frame. Sounds complicated, but with the kits available to build a lever frame making the task easier it is possible to operate the layout as the

Fig. 3.19

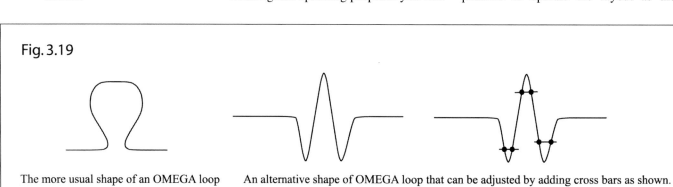

The more usual shape of an OMEGA loop

An alternative shape of OMEGA loop that can be adjusted by adding cross bars as shown. These will have the effect of reducing the flexibility of the loop.

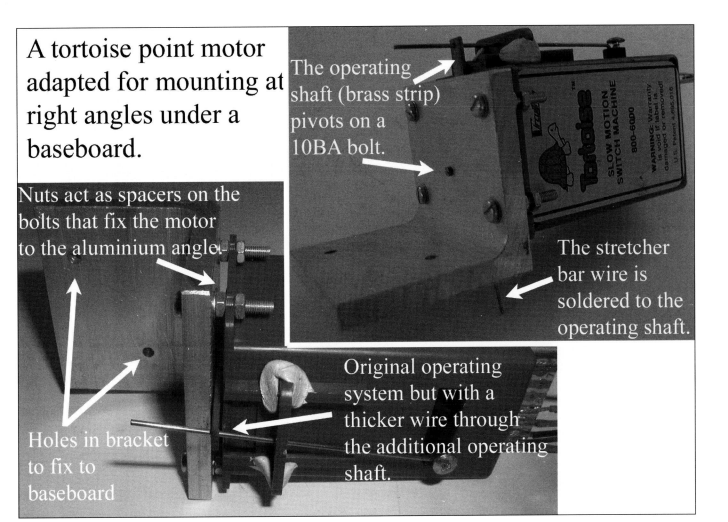

A tortoise point motor adapted for mounting at right angles under a baseboard.

The operating shaft (brass strip) pivots on a 10BA bolt.

The stretcher bar wire is soldered to the operating shaft.

Nuts act as spacers on the bolts that fix the motor to the aluminium angle.

Original operating system but with a thicker wire through the additional operating shaft.

Holes in bracket to fix to baseboard

prototype by using such a frame. Those who feel that is extra hassle can easily build a control panel and group the switches to operate the points together to represent such a frame. In this case electrical interlocking is possible. If you designed the layout using the *Trax* program you may have included a control panel incorporating a lever frame. The 'properties' you have allocated to each signal and point represent the electrical interlocking achievable with relays and thus prevent the incorrect actions on the panel and layout.

Mechanical interlocking is very easy to achieve using metal strips available from model shops, the hard part is working out the locking and applying it in practice. Levers within the frame operate a micro-switch that supplies the

relevant power to the point motors. Again the *Trax* program provides the interlocking in an electrical form that you need to convert to a mechanical set of rules. Most electric point motors have auxiliary switches built in that enable you to route signal power (assuming these are electrically operated also) through the point motor. Simple rule - if the point is wrong - the signal will not work!

If the panel or frame is located on a baseboard then mechanical connections can be made to the stretcher bars using the 'wire in tube' method. An omega loop (see fig 3.19) needs to be included in the run to allow for adjustments and to allow the lever or switch to have a throw slightly greater than that required to ensure the blades are held over properly. To carry the mechanical movement to an adjoining baseboard a spring loaded link

may be used. Electrical interlocking is still possible by adding a micro-switch somewhere in the operating wire route.

Another method used on layouts has been a double pole, double throw slide switch set into the baseboard top in line with the stretcher bar. The mechanical linkage is connected to the switch by drilling a small hole at right angles to the wire route through the switch. The electrical contacts provide the crossing vee power and still allow a spare set of contacts for those relays, lights, interlocking etc.

Point motors are of three main types.

1. Solenoid operation, e.g. H & M.
2. Slow acting motor operation, e.g. Lemaco, Fulgurex, Tortoise.
3. Memory wire, (not really a

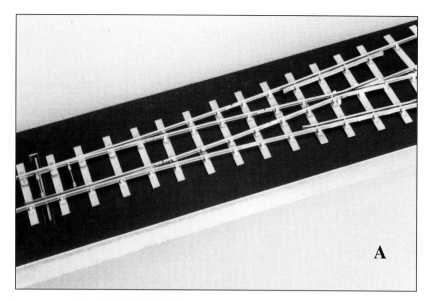

A

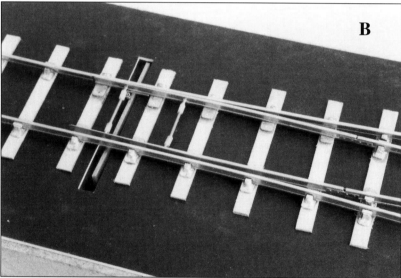

B

C

'motor' but needs power and so falls into this category).

Solenoid motors require a pulse of power.

A Capacitor Discharge Unit, (such as that described in *Wiring the Layout*), is recommended to enable them to function every time. The drawback with this type of motor is the sudden and harsh movement of the blades that can cause any soldered joint to fracture after continued use. The slow acting motors are by their very nature more gentle and can be powered by a DC power supply of up to 12 volts. Tortoise point motors have come on the scene more recently and operate on 9 volts DC very smoothly and quietly. All the above have two auxiliary switches, one of which can used to supply power to the crossing vee of the point. If the baseboard is built at least 4" (100mm) deep Tortoise motors may be mounted directly under the point. If this is not possible then a bracket is required to allow them to be fitted at right angles to their normal position.

Memory wire has more recently been used and is now available in kit form. The instructions with the kits need following carefully and their use in outdoor situations is still under trial owing to the fluctuations in temperature that can affect the amount of throw supplied to any stretcher bar. A personal objection here is the operation speed that is almost too slow for points especially on the return movement that relies on a spring and the wire cooling down sufficiently quickly.

The method of point operation, is, and will always be, a personal choice. You will need to bear in mind your ability to construct the system you choose and the finances available linked to the end goal of any additional interlocking.

Any choice of operation method will need to be born in mind when installing any point work. Baseboard supports under any point work may need to be avoided routes for wire in tube need to be routed in such a way so as to avoid other stretcher bars of point work. Holes in the baseboard to allow sufficient movement of any operating wire(s) may need drilling before finally installing the point.

ADVANCED TRACK CONSTRUCTION

This chapter looks at the more complex track formations, building on the experience gained from building a simple straight point in Chapter 3.

The techniques are the same, but the order of construction is important to ensure accurate trackwork that flows smoothly and looks great.

The illustrations commencing on the next page are all based on templates using the *Trax* program but are reduced in size to fit the page. Most have the sleeper spacing shown but do not go into great detail with this aspect as this has been covered in Chapter 3.

Above: Relaying near Cambridge in 1930 and with the aid of what was then a new cantilever truck which would pick up a complete section and transfer it to another truck before laying a replacement. The new length is then pulled into position using an electric winch.

Opposite page A-C.
'A' A metre gauge point built to a scale of 1:50 by Gordon Gravett. Because of the need to replicate chaired track, use has been made of 'S' Scale Society cast white metal chairs along with their Bullhead rail and Brook-Smith 4mm scale plywood sleepers. 'B' The chairs are bonded to the sleepers with slow setting Araldite which, although making it a slow process, results in very strong track. The blades pivot between nickel silver fishplates and the cosmetic wire tie-bars are insulated with pieces of plastic tube. Movement 'C' is transmitted by wire droppers that locate in pieces of brass tube soldered to a PCB sleeper mounted on edge.

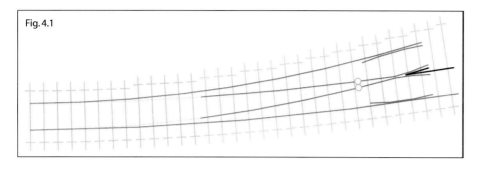

Fig. 4.1

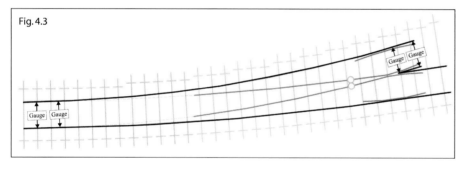

Fig. 4.2

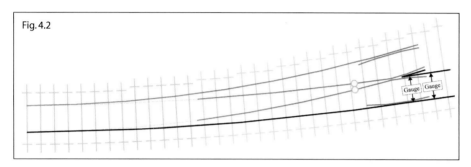

Fig. 4.3

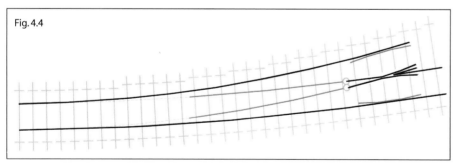

Fig. 4.4

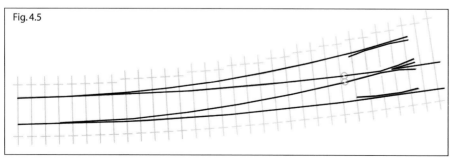

Fig. 4.5

Construction of a Curved Point

(Figs. 4.1 to 4.5.) Start a curved point by building the crossing vee. Here is a case for having the vee rails curved to match the rest of the point. Referring back to Chapter 3, lay the vee using the template as a guide.

With two gauges and having filed the recess in the stock rail for the blade (or bent the stock rail to produce the required joggle), lay the longer stock rail using the template as a guide.

Prepare the shorter stock rail and using gauges fix the stock rail at the forward end of the point ensuring the recesses in the stock rails are opposite each other. When set, move the gauges to the vee and ensure the rail follows the template.

Prepare and fit the wing rails, again using gauges. As you install each wing rail, run a wagon through the vee and check alignment with the vee.

Finally, fit the switch rails and check rails as explained in chapter 3.

An off-set scissors crossing seen at the approach to the 'down' platform in Coventry.

Fig. 4.6

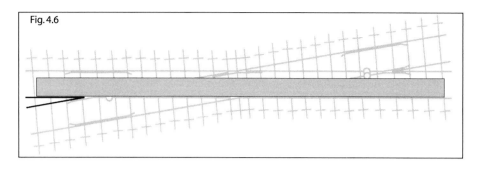

Fig. 4.7

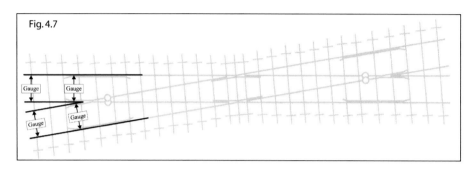

Fig. 4.8

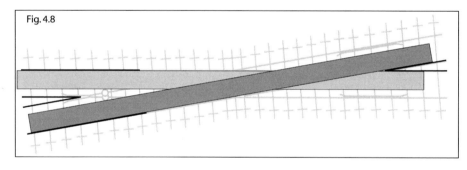

Fig. 4.9

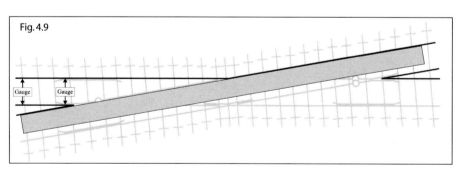

Fig. 4.10

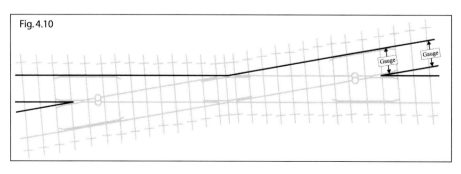

Construction of a Straight Diamond Crossing.

(Figs. 4.6 to 4.15.) Construction of this formation and any similar track with a straight section to it is made much easier with a metal track template at the correct gauge. These are available commercially. For the purposes of this book, we are assuming that you do not have access to such a template. You will need a straight edge instead.

Build a vee at the correct angle and install using a straight edge to check alignment with the template over the longer distance. Check in a similar way with the other route.

Using spare pieces of rail, fit temporary rails either side of the vee. Glue at least two chairs to the sleepers using gauges as shown. (These rails will be slid out of the chairs later, leaving the chairs to receive the correct rails.)

Fit the second vee using the straight edge against the temporary rails fitted in 4.7.

Prepare the elbow rail by bending

to the correct angle. Fit one part only, using gauges and the straight edge as shown. Ensure the bend is correctly positioned over the centre sleeper.

Fit the second half using gauges from the second vee.

The second elbow rail is fitted in a similar way. Keep checking with the straight edge and gauges to ensure accuracy.

Install the four wing rails as explained in chapter 3.

Having trimmed the wing rails so the length is equal, prepare the point rails. These need to be filed to the correct angle before cutting to length. Fit using a gauge to ensure the correct gap is left and check alignment with the straight edge. Once again check with a wagon.

Prepare and fit the obtuse checkrails at the centre of the crossing.

Finally prepare and fit the checkrails and fit the remaining half chairs where necessary.

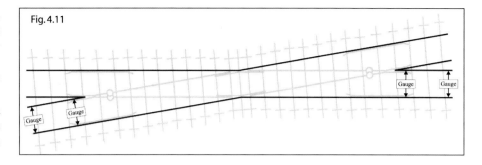
Fig. 4.11

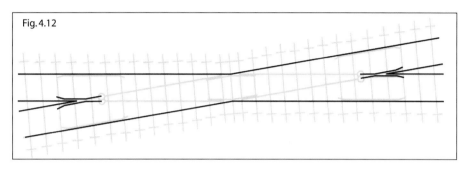
Fig. 4.12

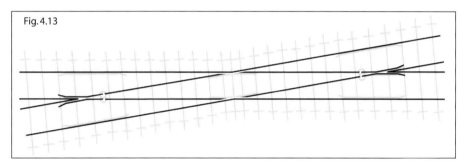
Fig. 4.13

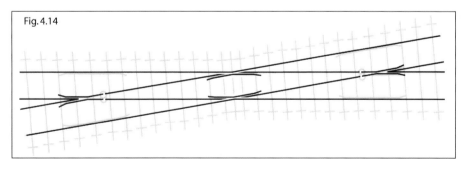
Fig. 4.14

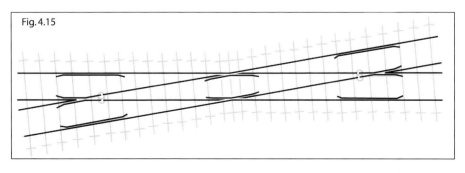
Fig. 4.15

Fig. 4.16

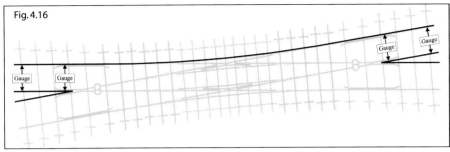

Fig. 4.17

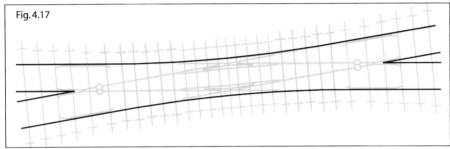

Fig. 4.18

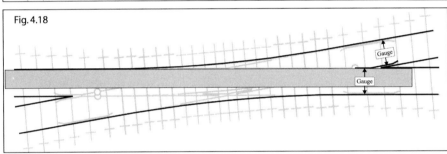

Fig. 4.19

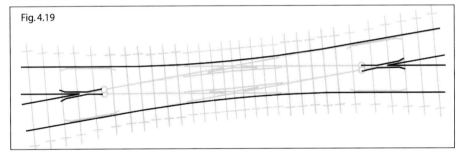

Construction of a Double (or Single) Slip

(Figs. 4.16 to 4.26.) These two items can be looked at together, in the case of the single slip omitting the rails and parts not required. Once again, this example is for a straight double slip and the use of a straight edge is essential. If the tracks forming the slip are curved, use your eye and the template to ensure a smooth curve throughout the slip.

Start by following the instructions in the previous section, figs 4.6. to 4.8. to fit the two vees for the slip.

With the vees correctly fitted, prepare the outer stock rails, taking care to introduce the joggle or file the recess for the switch rails where necessary. Using gauges as shown allow the stock rail to follow the template and fit. Remember to bend the stock rail slightly to allow the switch rail to fit closely to it as shown in chapter 3.

For double slips, fit the second stock rail in the same way. For single slips, fit the elbow rail as fig. 4.9 and 4.10.

Fit the first wing rail using a straight edge and gauges as shown.

Fit the remaining wing rails in a similar manner.

If using pre-made switchblades,

Below: The small section of rail highlighted, is about the minimum the modeller can cope with. Bear this in mind when designing your point work with TRAX.

arrange the joint for the elbow by carefully filing the end. Ensure the blade fits into the recess of the stock rails. Check alignment using two straight edges.

If building a double slip, repeat the above for the second elbow.

Using gauges and having prepared the recess for the switchblades, fit the inner point rails, remembering to file the correct angle where the rail meets the obtuse angle.

Fit the remaining inner point rails.

The curved switchblades can now be fitted. If using pre-made switchblades, arrange to join in the centre. Ensure the blades fit within the recess of the stock rails.

Fit the remaining switchblades.

Finally fit the obtuse checkrails. These may need trimming to fit behind the curved switch rails. The checkrails for the vees can also be fitted.

It is normal practice for all switchblades at one end to move together.

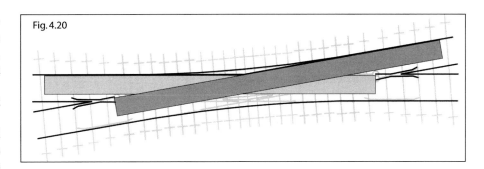

Fig. 4.20

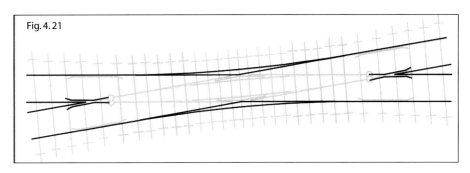

Fig. 4.21

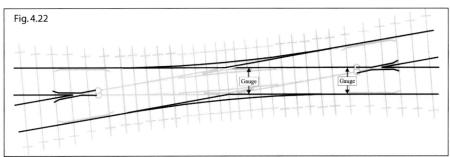

Fig. 4.22

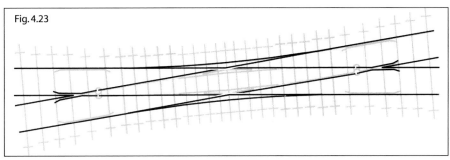

Fig. 4.23

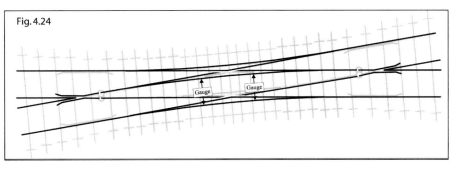

Fig. 4.24

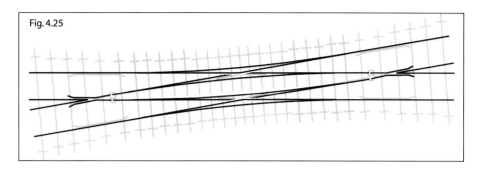

Fig. 4.25

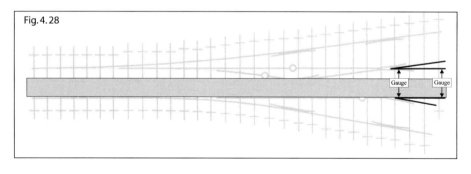

Fig. 4.26

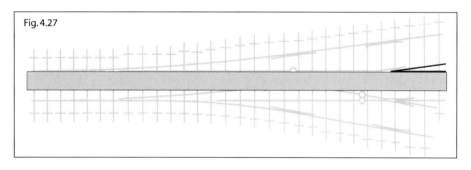

Fig. 4.27

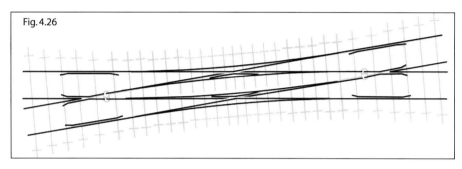

Fig. 4.28

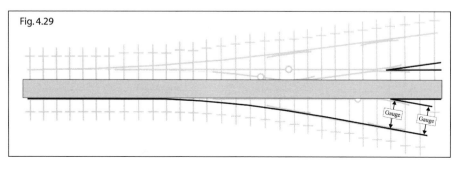

Fig. 4.29

Construction of a three Way Point

(Figs. 4.27 to 4.39.) Assuming the three-way point has a main straight track, straight edges can be used for alignment. If all roads are curved, then the eye and the template are your guide.

Prepare and lay the first vee using a straight edge to align with the template.

Using gauges and the straight edge, lay the second vee.

Choosing the curved stock rail that has two recesses to accept the two switch rails, prepare and lay using gauges and the straight edge.

Prepare the other stock rail and ensure the recess is opposite the other stock rail fitted at the forward end of the point. Move the gauges to the vee and fit the stock rail aligning to the template.

As the point has a straight road, lay the first wing rail for that road as a straight edge may be used to assist with alignment. Note the wing rail lengths are not always equal.

Prepare and lay the second wing rail for the straight road.

Now continue to fit the second wing rail to the vee using gauges as shown.

Fit the fourth wing rail as shown.

Prepare and lay the third vee. The *Trax* template and gauges will help to produce the correct angles.

Using gauges fit and lay the wing rails for the third vee.

Prepare the first switch rail and fit.

Prepare the second switch rail that also acts as a stock rail. File a recess in it ensuring it is opposite the other recess.

Fit the last two switch rails. Finally fit the checkrails. The *Trax* template will show where it is considered necessary to join two checkrails together to form one long checkrail.

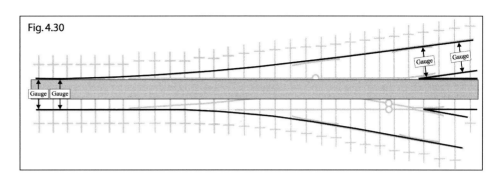

Fig. 4.30

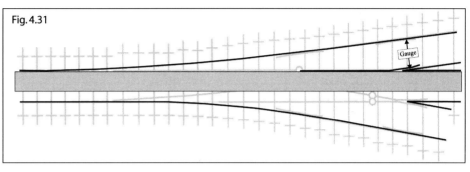

Fig. 4.31

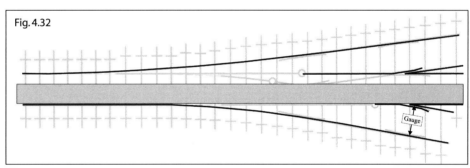

Fig. 4.32

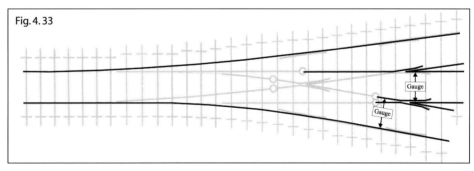

Fig. 4.33

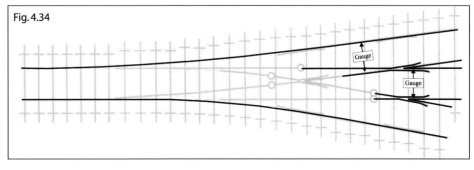

Fig. 4.34

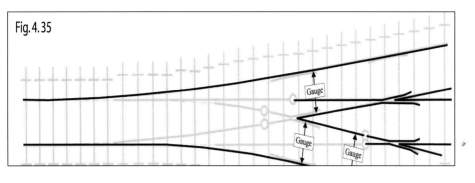

Fig. 4.35

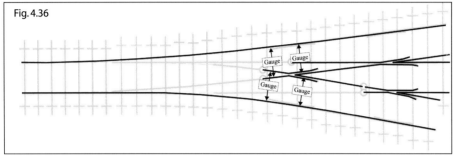

Fig. 4.36

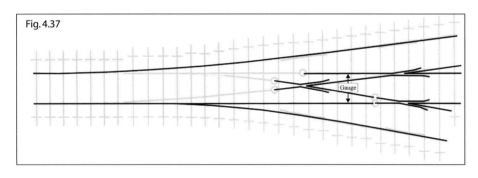

Fig. 4.37

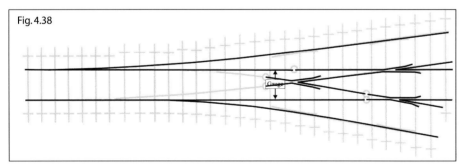

Fig. 4.38

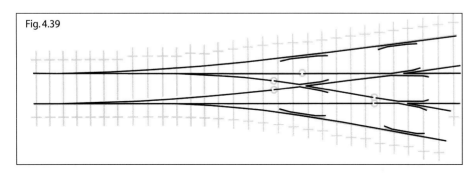

Fig. 4.39

Chapter 5

FIDDLE YARDS and STORAGE SIDINGS

Introduction

All layouts need some form of storage space for stock not in use on the scenic part of the layout. When space is at a premium, it is hard to have to provide such space at the cost of losing part of the layout, which at the end of the day is your prime objective. Storage space can take up twice the space for a small through station as of course space is needed both ends. Some very clever and ingenious space saving designs of storage have been used; below is a sample of some of them. One important consideration is the ability to change trains off stage without actually handling the stock with your hands.

All the examples shown are drawn to the same scale in the same overall length. Compare how different designs allow longer trains to be stored and perhaps greater flexibility of use.

Storage Sidings and Loops

Storage sidings and loops are possibly the simplest form of storage but can take up more space than other methods, as point work needs to be included to provide the various options. Space around the points can of course be used for other purposes such as controllers or other stock storage.

Fig 5.1 shows a set of loops for a fiddle yard where access is required at both ends, e.g. a circular layout. Notice how the loop lengths all vary. This can be a problem if more than one train is being used on the scenic part of the layout, as it may be too long for the vacant loop left. Notice also how points swallow up space and do not provide storage. The sidings method, however, is the easiest to produce as standard or complex points may be built and operated by the same methods as the main layout. Some form of detection system together with route setting will enable the modeller to operate the fiddle yard without leaving the main control position until locos need moving etc.

In Fig 5.2 the loop lengths are all the same, about the same length as the second longest in fig 5.2. At least now the operator need not worry which train

fits into which loop.

Fig 5.3 shows a fiddle yard for an 'end to end' layout. The central siding is the longest but by only using simple point work the sidings are different lengths.

By building your own points designed with the *Trax* programme it is possible to have more sidings the same length as shown in fig 5.4. A cassette has been shown at the end of the sidings, the length "X" representing the longest locomotive likely to grace the layout. The length "X" is also shown at the start of the fiddle yard to allow a locomotive to be run-round its train using an empty siding before rejoining its train and still stay out of view of the scenic layout. This arrangement takes up a little more space as each siding, from its stock clearance point, needs to hold a locomotive and the train without using the cassette. Locomotive exchanges can be arranged by including double slips in place of the two straight points. See fig 5.5. where the cassette is used to transfer the locomotive to the front of the sidings.

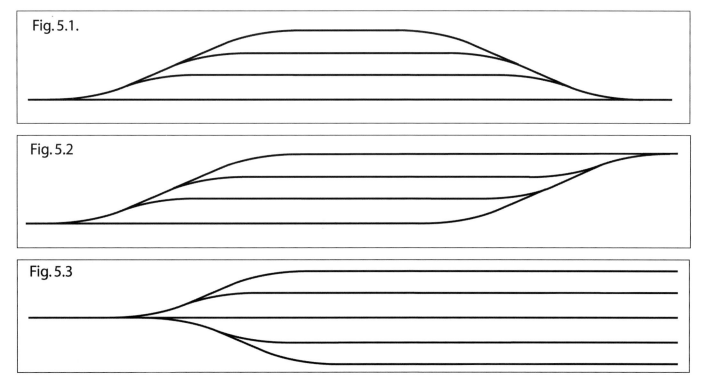

Fig. 5.1.

Fig. 5.2

Fig. 5.3

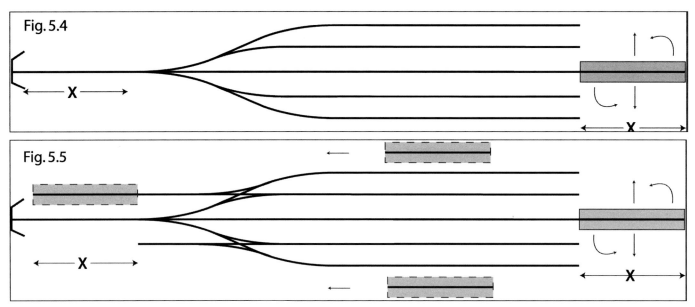

Fig. 5.4

Fig. 5.5

Traversers

Traversers are basically a sliding set of tracks that can each line up with a running road in turn. Traversers can be single ended or double ended and can therefore be used in circular layouts. Some skills are required to build such a feature but with accessories now available from model suppliers, the task is a little easier. Some form of electrical connection between the approach road and the chosen traverser road is needed, usually taking the form of sliding bolts that lock the traverser in position also. The number of storage roads is limited to the safe overhang permitted when pushed to its extreme.

Note how in fig 5.6 the width of the fiddle yard chassis needs to be greater to allow the traverser to service all the tracks. If the layout is at home against a wall, this needs to be considered. Again use is made of a cassette for moving/turning locomotives.

Sector Plates

A sector plate is a traverser pivoted one end. The same requirements need to be met re alignment and electrical connections to the running tracks. It is only of use when in an 'end to end' situation although it is possible to build one that when in the centre position allows trains to run through the sector plate to a further baseboard or second station. The tracks need to be curved at their ends to meet the fixed track at right angles and this takes up a little space as shown in fig 5.7.

Cassettes

Cassettes are quite new to the hobby and again some very sophisticated methods of alignment and electrical connections have been devised. The basic requirements are two strips of angle, (usually aluminium) available from good D.I.Y. stores fixed at the appropriate gauge to a length of timber. Care - do NOT buy anodised aluminium, as this does not conduct electricity!

Fig 5.8 is drawn to the same scale as fig 5.6, but note how the cassettes are longer than the traverser. A short lead in to the cassette is required to provide alignment and electrical connections off scene. By shuffling around the cassettes on a flat smooth surface there is no need to lift filled cassettes, only empty ones.

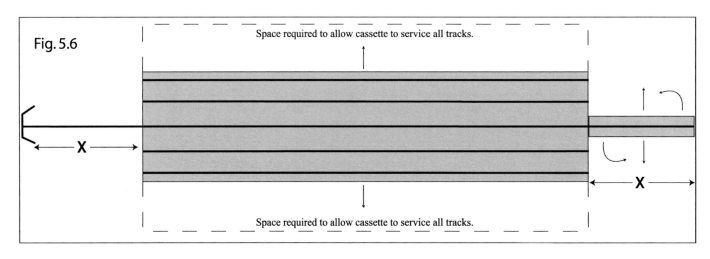

Fig. 5.6

Space required to allow cassette to service all tracks.

Space required to allow cassette to service all tracks.

Fig. 5.7

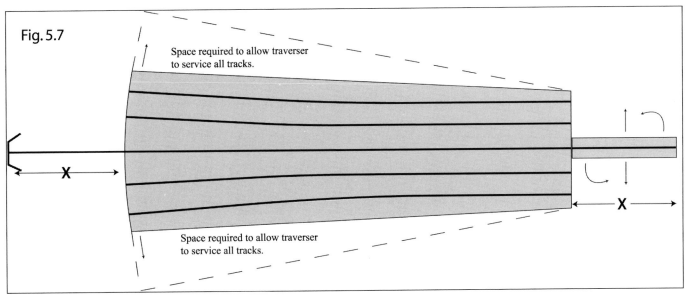

Space required to allow traverser to service all tracks.

Space required to allow traverser to service all tracks.

X

X

Fig. 5.8

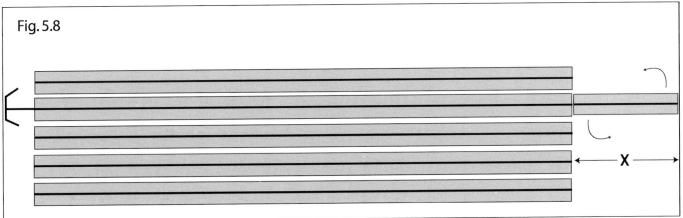

X

A prototype storage yard. The concrete pot sleepers is a feature rarely modelled.

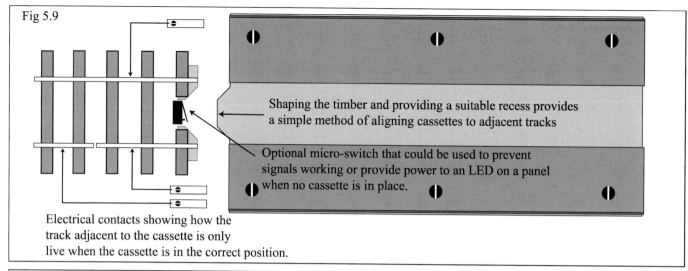

Fig 5.9

Shaping the timber and providing a suitable recess provides a simple method of aligning cassettes to adjacent tracks

Optional micro-switch that could be used to prevent signals working or provide power to an LED on a panel when no cassette is in place.

Electrical contacts showing how the track adjacent to the cassette is only live when the cassette is in the correct position.

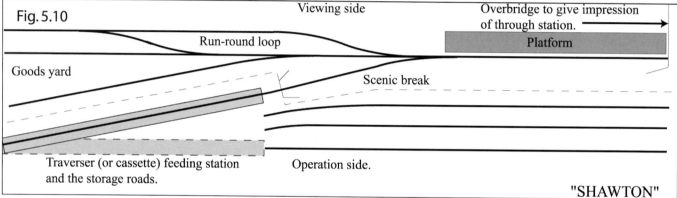

Fig. 5.10

Viewing side

Overbridge to give impression of through station.

Run-round loop

Platform

Goods yard

Scenic break

Traverser (or cassette) feeding station and the storage roads.

Operation side.

"SHAWTON"

Alignment need only be two bulldog clips to a similar fixed length of aluminium track.

Fig 5.9 shows a simple alternative alignment method and also a safe way of transferring power to the cassette. If there is no cassette in place, the approach track to the fiddle yard is electrically dead and prevents a train dropping into the space where the cassette should be. The micro-switch is an additional feature that allows signals to be interlocked or an LED on the panel to show whether a cassette is in place or not.

Fig 5.10 shows a very small layout design that needs careful planning to work properly. The drawing is not to scale but the critical measurements must ensure that:

1. A loco and its train fit in the platform clear of the point.
2. The same train must fit onto the traverser and storage roads.
3. The coaches or goods vehicles must be able to stand in the loop allowing the loco to run-round.

The fiddle yard is behind the scenic part and does not add additional length to the overall layout. The layout can be extended at a later date by adding track at the overbridge.

Fig 5.11 develops the above but

requires two traversers to feed a through station. The traversers can be hidden by scenic extensions to the layout.

Control of the Fiddle Yard

Whatever method of control you use for the scenic and main part of the layout, ensure you provide sufficient space for similar controls for the fiddle yard. If you choose to have a lever frame with working signals, include a fiddle yard Starter signal and a Home signal in the plan, even if these are represented by LED's instead of modelled signals. If on leaving the fiddle yard there is a choice of route, say platform or goods loop, showing a junction signal as the Starter will indicate clearly to the local operator which sort of train is to be dispatched next.

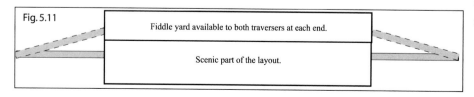

Fig. 5.11

Fiddle yard available to both traversers at each end.

Scenic part of the layout.

Chapter 6

USING *TRAX 2*

As has been mentioned in previous chapters, *Trax 2* has been designed to include facilities useful to track builders. There are two main areas in which these facilities can help. The first of these is in allowing you to design and to some extent even test the track plan, in a sense to develop a 'virtual' railway on the computer. This will allow you to check things like clearances, minimum radii, whether your platforms and sidings are long enough for the trains you wish to run, and so on. The second area in which *Trax 2* can be invaluable is the printing of templates on which you can build your track. There are several commercial sources of templates for this purpose, however for obvious reasons it would not be feasible for the makers of these to supply every possible track formation off the shelf. Using *Trax 2* allows you to design a very specific piece of track, for example a curved or three-way point with radii and angles exactly suited to your layout requirements.

There is a third area in which the computer can be useful, though it is not covered in this book. A companion volume, *Wiring the Layout* described how *Trax* can be used to design and test your layout wiring strategy to ensure that there are no short circuits or dead sections. The book also described how a layout can be operated entirely by a signal box type lever frame. In this scheme, it is the signals that control the electrical circuits on the track, rather than a bank of switches. Routes must be set up, and signals cleared appropriately, before any train can move. Great satisfaction can be obtained by running your railway in this highly realistic way. For details of how to use the electrical capabilities of *Trax*, the interested reader is referred to *Wiring the Layout.*

If you have already purchased *Wiring the Layout,* and are familiar with *Trax,* you might find it useful to look at the 'what's new' file on the *Trax 2* CD. This will highlight a number of innovations and changes in the way certain things are done.

Trax Templates

We will first consider the printing of templates for track construction. There are a number of things you should note about *Trax* templates. The first is a general point about the way in which the geometry and sleeper spacing is calculated. Each railway company had its own permanent way department, and although they all worked to the same track gauge and general principles of construction there were differences in details. *Trax* does not attempt to reproduce any one railway's trackwork precisely. Rather, it uses a set of fairly typical rules to space sleepers and other features so that the track looks reasonably representative of virtually any standard gauge railway.

For example, when calculating the geometry of a standard point, *Trax* will place a number of sleepers under the switch blades according to the switch length. These sleepers will be colour-coded to indicate that they carry slide chairs rather than ordinary chairs. The centre-line of the first sleeper will be placed a scale 4" forward of the end of the switch blades and the last a scale 1' 1" back from the joint (for old-type blades) or the start of the flexible portion of the switch (for later flexible switches). The remaining slide chair sleepers will be positioned equally between these two. *Trax* will then calculate the lead of the point, that is, the distance from the toe of the switch to the intersection point of the crossing vee. A sleeper will be placed with its centre-line 4" forward of the nose of the vee, and a number of sleepers positioned equally between this and the last of the slide chair sleepers. The number is determined such that these sleepers are approximately 2' 3" apart.

As the turnout stock rail diverges, the sleeper length required will obviously increase. *Trax* works out how long a sleeper would be required at each position, then sets the actual length to an appropriate multiple of 6", this being the way most railway sleepers were supplied.

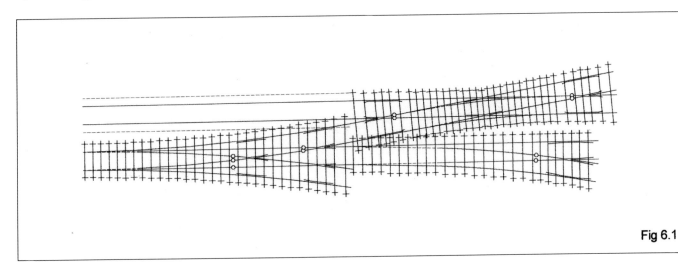

Fig 6.1

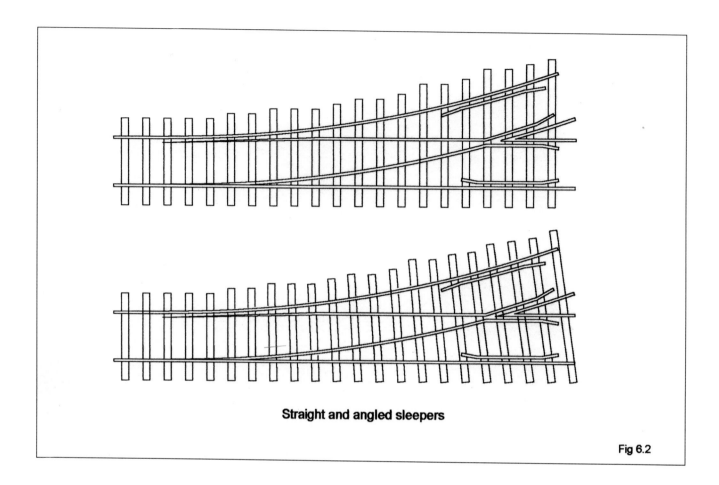

Straight and angled sleepers

Fig 6.2

Similar sets of rules are applied to diamond crossings, single and double slips etc. The result is, we hope, reasonably representative. However, for the modeller who is determined to have everything exactly as per the prototype, specific information, such as timbering diagrams for the railway in question, must be sought out.

Printing Templates

When printing templates, *Trax* takes a slightly different approach from the commercially produced templates that are available. In effect, the template is simply a zoomed-in view of a part of the layout. It may encompass one or more individual track parts, such as points or slips, or in the larger scales it may only be possible to fit a part of a point on one sheet of paper.

This approach is taken because, when points and crossings are built adjacent to each other, their sleepers may interfere with each other. For example, figure 6.1 - previous page, shows some points and a single slip joined together. Where they join, several sleepers clash. As with the prototype, some judgement must be exercised by the builder. Maybe you would choose to move the sleeper positions slightly to allow them to interlace, or you might prefer to replace all of them by sleepers going straight across both lines. *Trax* cannot do this itself, but by printing them as shown it does at least draw your attention to the need for some corrective action.

To print the template, we need first of all to set up our printer in either landscape or portrait mode, as preferred, and select 'Show Sleepers' from the Options menu. Then, on the 'Miscellaneous' toolbar, we use the page size tool to place a rectangle on the track plan which represents the printable area of a sheet of paper (this is generally smaller than the paper size because of

your printer's need to hold the paper whilst printing). You can move this around with the hand tool until it is in the correct location. Further pages can be added, until the required area of the layout is covered. Then, simply press the print button, or select the File/Print menu item, to bring up the print dialog box and select the Templates option.

Trax will then print an actual size template for the track part(s) selected. To work out the size, *Trax* uses your printer driver software to find out how many dots represent one inch, and scales the picture accordingly. However, a word of caution is appropriate. Not all printers have absolutely accurate registration, and sometimes the dots per inch figures are rather more nominal than might be hoped. Also, like many drawing programs, *Trax* approximates curves by drawing a number of successive straight lines. Therefore, the template you produce from Trax is a *guide only*. Do not use it to line up rails by eye. An accurate track gauge is essential equipment, and this should be used for actually positioning your rail.

On the template, sleepers are represented by a long line, which is their centre-line, and two short lines at right angles, which represent the ends of the sleeper. They are aligned with the 'straight on' direction for points. Some railways, notably the Great Western, aligned sleepers at right angles to the arc through the central crossing vee, as shown in figure 6.2. Again, if you wish to follow your chosen prototype's practise exactly, you will need to research this point.

Creating Custom Track Parts

Trax has built-in capability to calculate the geometry of a wide range of track parts such as left and right hand points, Y points, curved points, three way points, diamond crossings, single and double slips and catch points. However, there may be a requirement on your layout for a configuration that is not included. For example, if you wanted to build a double track junction on a curve, you would need a diamond crossing in which both legs were curved to different radii. *Trax* only draws diamonds with straight legs.

For help with producing such track parts, the alignment tool will be found invaluable. We saw in chapter 1 (figure 1.9) how the alignment tool could be used to create a partial template for a curved diamond crossing. We call this a partial template because it contains only the running faces of the main rails. The builder will have to pencil in the appropriate check rails and wing rails, and work out sleeper locations etc. However, once a little experience has been obtained in building standard track parts, these should present no problem.

When you use the alignment tool in this way, you may find it difficult to select the aligner for joining up rather than a length of track already joined to it. It can be done, if you click within the aligner rectangle, but outside the gauge

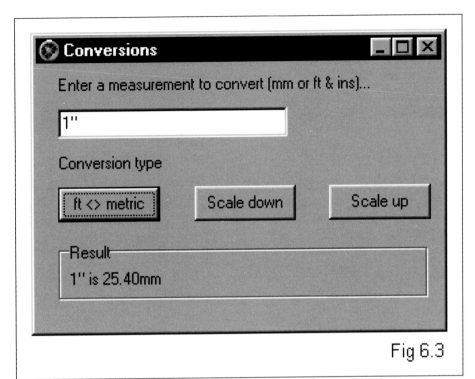

Fig 6.3

of the track. However, unless you are zoomed right in, this is not easy. *Trax* will bring up the Multiple Parts Selected dialog box in such cases, showing all the parts which it thinks you might mean to indicate. Select the appropriate one by using the up and down arrow keys, then hit return.

The Tools Menu

Under the Tools menu item, you will find a variety of useful tools which will be of value during track design. These include a conversion utility, which allows you to convert measurements from metric to feet and inches and vice versa, and calculators to help you establish whether particular vehicles will go round tight curves, and whether your tracks are sufficiently far apart.

Conversion Utility

Figure 6.3 illustrates the *Trax* conversion utility. This allows you to enter a measurement in either metres, millimetres or feet and inches, and to convert it. *Trax* will work out from what you have typed which conversion is required. If you enter a figure with no units, *Trax* assumes these are

millimetres.

Below the edit box are three buttons. The first does a straight conversion. Thus if you type 1" in the edit box, the result will be 25.40mm. If you type 25.4mm the result will be given as 1.000 inches.

The second button scales down the measurement you have typed according to the layout scale (note that for this reason you cannot use the conversion utility until a layout has been set up). Thus if you are using 7mm/ft scale, you enter 20ft in the edit box and click the 'scale down' button, the result will be 140.00mm. That is, 20 feet on the prototype is represented by 140mm on the model.

The third button scales the other way. The measurement you type in is assumed to be an actual measurement on the model, and if you click the 'scale up' button, the result will tell you what this measurement on the model represents in real life.

Minimum Radius Calculator

The minimum radius calculator, shown in figure 6.4, has already been described in chapter 2, where the

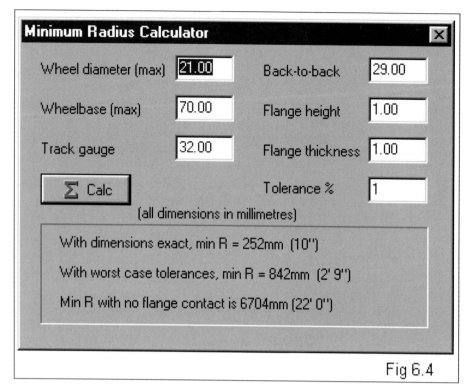

Minimum Radius Calculator

Wheel diameter (max)   21.00   Back-to-back   29.00

Wheelbase (max)   70.00   Flange height   1.00

Track gauge   32.00   Flange thickness   1.00

Σ Calc   Tolerance %   1

(all dimensions in millimetres)

With dimensions exact, min R = 252mm (10")

With worst case tolerances, min R = 842mm (2' 9")

Min R with no flange contact is 6704mm (22' 0")

Fig 6.4

geometry of track and wheels was discussed. As was mentioned in that chapter, there are several different interpretations of 'minimum radius'. The absolute minimum, below which a vehicle could not even be placed on the track with its tread touching the rail head is not really acheivable in practice. The calculator allows you to see the effect of errors in wheel alignment, track gauge, etc. Normally, you should allow at least 1% tolerance, and this will give you a more realistic radius that might be usable.

At the other end of the scale, the minimum radius that your vehicles could negotiate without contact between flange and rail running face is generally much too large to work to in any practical layout.

Of course, you will want to set different minimum radii for your goods yard, main line, branch lines etc, depending on the type of traffic to be accomodated. If your goods sidings are unlikely to be occupied by anything other than short wheelbase wagons, then they

can have a much tighter radius than a main line, where you might want to run longer vehicles.

It should be understood that in the context of minimum radius calculations, what counts is the *fixed* wheelbase. For example a bogie coach with two 7ft wheelbase bogies, 43 ft apart has a fixed wheelbase of 7ft, not 50ft as might be thought. Similarly, for a 2-6-4 locomotive what is important is the wheelbase of the central 6 wheels. Because the bogie and pony truck are able to move laterally, they will not restrict the radius the engine can negotiate.

Clearance Calculator

With long bogie coaches on tight curves, however, a second factor comes into play. This is the overhang between the bogies on the inside of the curve, and the overhang of the ends of the vehicle on the outside of the curve, as illustrated in figure 6.5. When two bogie coaches pass each other on a curve, these overhangs can result in a collision if the tracks are too close together.

The standard distance between tracks, called the *interval,* is one of the parameters you set up when you start a new layout. It is used, among other things, to determine the length of turnout curves on points and crossings so that two identical points joined back-to-back will give exactly the right separation to form a crossover.

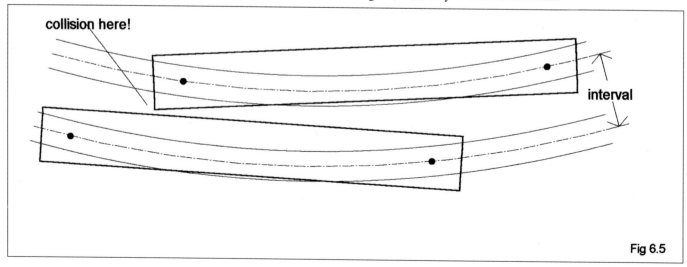

collision here!

interval

Fig 6.5

This distance on the prototype is generally just over 11 feet. Prototype vehicles are rarely more than 9 ft 6 ins wide, so that there is ample clearance between vehicles on adjacent tracks. However, on a curve the overhangs come into play. If the curve is tight, or if the vehicle is extra long or wide then the overhangs may reach so far that they exceed the standard interval between tracks.

The clearance calculator, illustrated in figure 6.6, will alert you to this possibility. You may then wish to increase the separation of tracks on the more tightly curved sections of the layout to avoid the possibility of collisions.

Curve Calculator

We saw in chapter 2 how important it is that, when two curves of different radius are joined, they must have a common tangent at the junction point. This is only acheived if the junction and their respective centres of curvature lie

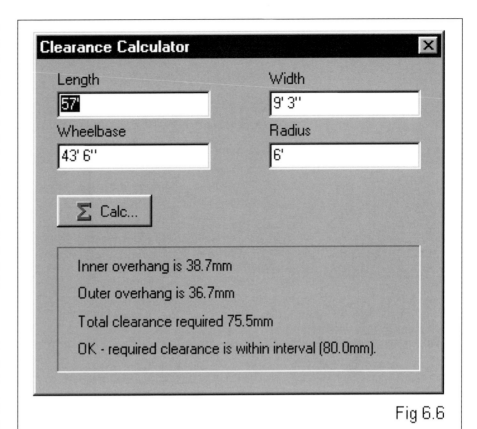

Fig 6.6

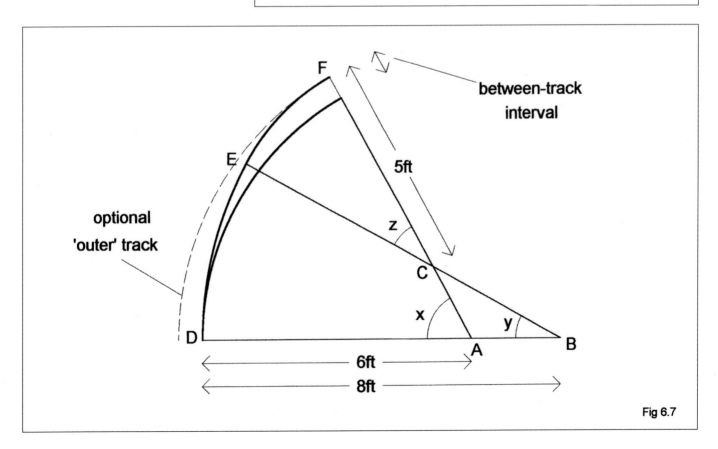

Fig 6.7

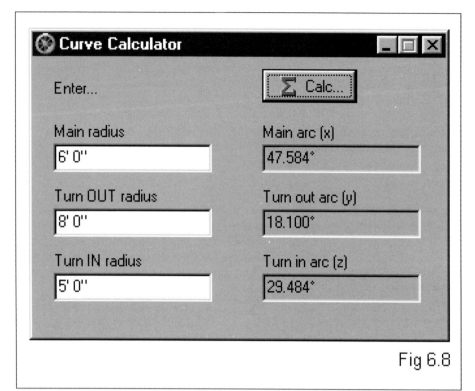

Fig 6.8

on the same straight line. When designing curved points, you must ensure that this condition is met. The Curve Calculator tool enables you to do this.

As an example, let us design a right-hand curved point to take a single line of 6ft radius out to a pair of parallel lines one standard interval apart. One way of doing this would be to set up a curved point that looked 'about right' then join it up to an appropriately sized spacer using flexible track. However, such an approach could lead to a hotch-potch of straights and curves of different radii. Far better to design it with the minimum number of changes of radius using the curve calculator.

Referring to figure 6.7, we have illustrated a curved right-hand point. For clarity, only the centre lines of the track are shown. The inner track is of radius 6ft, and its centre is at point A. The outer track, of radius 8ft, starts at the same location, D, and has its centre at B. As we move round the curve, these two tracks diverge. At some location, labelled E in figure 6.7, we need to change the radius of the outer track from one that is *larger* than the inner radius to

one that is *smaller*, so that after a while the 'new' outer arc and our original 6ft curve will be both exactly one standard interval apart, and exactly parallel. We have labelled this location F. Suppose we choose 5ft as this smaller radius. Our problem boils down to this: exactly where should we locate the change of radius in the outer curve (i.e. point E) so that when the tracks draw parallel they are exactly one interval apart? In other words, we need the angles labelled x, y and z in figure 6.7.

Because of the requirement for a common tangent at changes of radius, we know that points A, B and D must lie on the same line, and likewise points B, C and E. We also require the exits to be parallel so points A, C and F must be in line as well. Now, if you happen to remember enough of your school geometry, this gives you the necessary information to solve triangle ABC and thus work out the angles x, y and z. Alternatively, you can simply type the three radii into the Curve Calculator, press the calculate button, and read off the answers!

You can now set up a curved point

using the curved point tool on the Track palette, then right-click to bring up its properties box. Selecting the 'curved point' tab, set radii 6ft and 8ft, uncheck the 'end curve at check rail' box and instead continue the curves through angles 47.58° and 18.10° respectively (figure 6.8). This will give you a curved point which can then be joined up with flexible track and a spacer to create the track formation we require as in figure 6.9.

Function Keys

The function keys allow short cuts to various frequently-used menu selections. Once you have become familiar with them, they will enable you to design and check a layout in the shortest possible time. The function key short-cuts are as follows.

F1 *Help* - pressing F1 at any time brings up the *Trax* help file.

F2 *Parts List* - pressing F2 brings up the Parts List dialog box. You can select various different types of list, including a list of tight curves, short lengths of track, all operating parts, etc.

F3 *Sleepers* - press F3 to include sleepers in the layout drawing. Normally, only the running faces of track are shown to avoid clutter. If you are printing a template, then you will wish to show sleeper positions, so use F3. On points and slips, the sleepers will be colour-coded to indicate which sleepers support slide chairs and which support ordinary chairs. On plain track, individual sleepers are not shown. Instead, a dashed line indicates the sleeper ends. You should position sleepers according to the rail lengths you wish to represent. The same applies to very long curved points.

F4 *Clearance Lines* - press F4 to show the extent either side of the track of a 9 ft 6ins wide vehicle at the scale of your layout. As noted in chapter 2, for long vehicles on sharp curves, the overhang should be allowed for also. (see Clearances Calculator, above). Note that the colour coding used for sleepers, clearance lines, etc. can be changed by using the Options/Drawing Preferences menu item.

F5 *Refresh* - *Trax* does not redraw the entire layout every time you make a change. It only redraws the changed part, first in the background colour (white) to erase it, then in the appropriate foreground colour with changes applied. Eventually, after many such partial redrawings, the layout may become a little untidy. Press F5 to completely redraw it from scratch.

F6 *Show Grid Lines* - If you defined your layout size in feet and inches, pressing F6 will give you a series of dotted lines at one foot intervals on both the control panel and the layout. If you used metres or millimetres, the grid line spacing will be 500mm. As with F3 and F4, this shortcut is a toggle. If gridlines are already showing, this will turn them off.

F7 *Snap to Grid* - If grid lines are shown on the control panel, pressing F7 will cause mouse positions to 'snap' to the nearest inch or 25mm depending on the grid units. This is useful for positioning

controls such as switches in a straight line. To get the same effect on the layout, hold down the shift key whilst pressing F7. To remind you that the snap facility is operative, *Trax* redraws the dotted grid lines as solid.

F8 *Hide Alignment Tools* - The alignment tool is not a part of a layout, but a device for helping design one. Unlike the spacer tool, however, you will not normally want to delete it, as this would leave track part ends unconnected. Use F8 to hide any alignment tools when you want to print your layout. When printing a template, you might also want to hide signals, labels and buildings. To do this, hold down the shift key whilst pressing F8.

F9 *Test Mode* - F9 toggles between test mode and design mode. In design mode you can add, change and delete individual components of your layout, and set up their electrical properties. In test mode, you can operate the dynamic parts of your layout such as points, levers, toggle switches etc. and see the effect on the layout electrical circuits. Full details are given in *Wiring the Layout*.

F10 *Reset* - F10 is only functional in test mode. Pressing it will restore all switches, levers, and other moving parts to their initial settings as specified in their Properties dialog box. Use this to recover from short circuit conditions etc.

F11 *Colour Code Circuits* - F11 is again only functional in test mode. It toggles on and off the colour-coding of track to indicate which controller (if any) it is connected to.

F12 *Show Track Single* - pressing F12 will show track as a single line, rather than showing the two running faces of the rails. This can be useful for printing track plans for use in making up signal box diagrams etc.

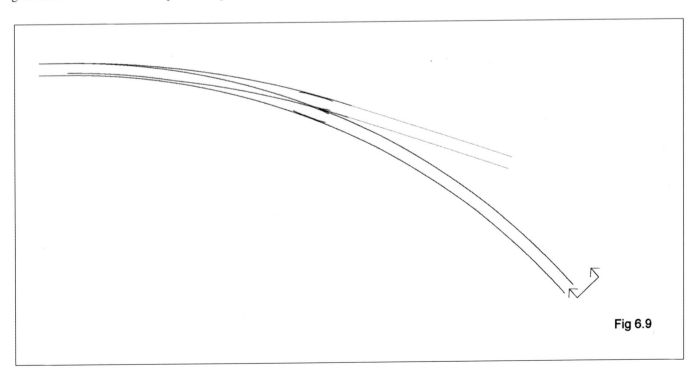

Fig 6.9

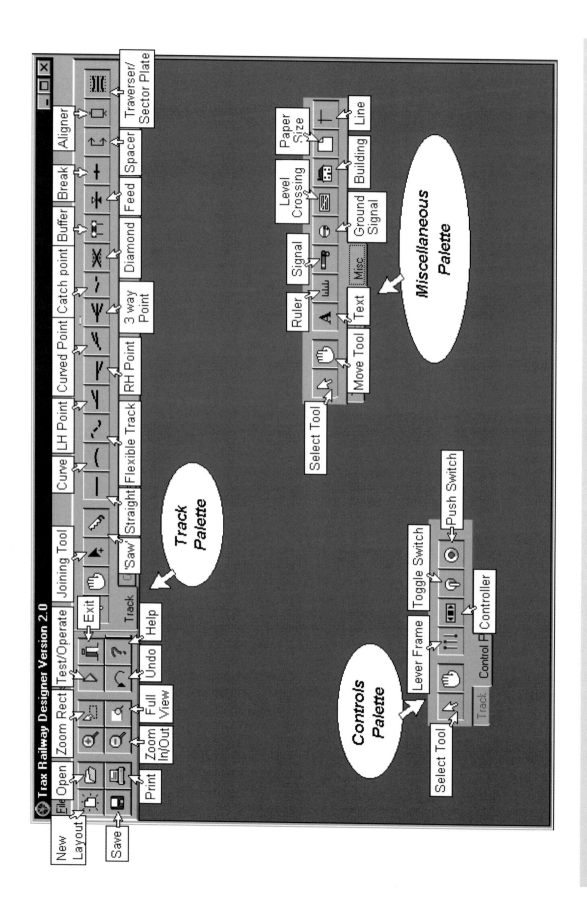

Conversion of Angles

For an angle described as 1 in N, by Right Angle Measure (see figure 2.8) the value in degrees is given by A = *arctan*(1/N).
For Centre Line Measure, it is A = *2arctan*(0.5/N).
and for Isosceles Measure, it is A = *2arcsin*(0.5/N).
Where the angle is described by true angular measure, i.e. the ratio of arc length to radius as in figure 2.9, then A = 180/(Nπ.)
The value in degrees of angles described as 1 in N by each of these measures is given in the table below, together with the error, also in degrees, of approximating twice the angle by halving N.

N	RAM	error	CLM	error	IM	error	AM	error
2	26.565	8.130	28.072	3.015	28.955	-2.090	28.648	0.000
2.5	21.801	4.943	22.620	1.637	23.074	-1.009	22.918	0.000
3	18.435	3.180	18.925	0.979	19.188	-0.566	19.099	0.000
3.5	15.945	2.146	16.260	0.630	16.426	-0.350	16.370	0.000
4	14.036	1.507	14.250	0.428	14.362	-0.232	14.324	0.000
4.5	12.529	1.095	12.680	0.303	12.759	-0.162	12.732	0.000
5	11.310	0.818	11.421	0.223	11.478	-0.117	11.459	0.000
5.5	10.305	0.627	10.389	0.168	10.432	-0.088	10.417	0.000
6	9.462	0.490	9.527	0.130	9.560	-0.067	9.549	0.000
6.5	8.746	0.390	8.797	0.102	8.823	-0.053	8.815	0.000
7	8.130	0.315	8.171	0.082	8.192	-0.042	8.185	0.000
7.5	7.595	0.258	7.628	0.067	7.645	-0.034	7.639	0.000
8	7.125	0.214	7.153	0.055	7.167	-0.028	7.162	0.000
8.5	6.710	0.179	6.733	0.046	6.745	-0.024	6.741	0.000
9	6.340	0.152	6.360	0.039	6.369	-0.020	6.366	0.000
9.5	6.009	0.129	6.026	0.033	6.034	-0.017	6.031	0.000
10	5.711	0.111	5.725	0.028	5.732	-0.014	5.730	0.000
10.5	5.440	0.096	5.453	0.025	5.459	-0.012	5.457	0.000
11	5.194	0.084	5.205	0.021	5.211	-0.011	5.209	0.000
11.5	4.970	0.074	4.979	0.019	4.984	-0.009	4.982	0.000
12	4.764	0.065	4.772	0.016	4.776	-0.008	4.775	0.000
12.5	4.574	0.058	4.581	0.015	4.585	-0.007	4.584	0.000
13	4.399	0.051	4.405	0.013	4.408	-0.007	4.407	0.000
13.5	4.236	0.046	4.242	0.012	4.245	-0.006	4.244	0.000
14	4.086	0.041	4.091	0.010	4.093	-0.005	4.093	0.000
14.5	3.945	0.037	3.950	0.009	3.952	-0.005	3.951	0.000
15	3.814	0.034	3.818	0.008	3.820	-0.004	3.820	0.000
15.5	3.691	0.030	3.695	0.008	3.697	-0.004	3.697	0.000
16	3.576	0.028	3.580	0.007	3.582	-0.004	3.581	0.000
16.5	3.468	0.025	3.471	0.006	3.473	-0.003	3.472	0.000
17	3.366	0.023	3.369	0.006	3.371	-0.003	3.370	0.000
17.5	3.270	0.021	3.273	0.005	3.274	-0.003	3.274	0.000
18	3.180	0.019	3.182	0.005	3.184	-0.002	3.183	0.000
18.5	3.094	0.018	3.096	0.005	3.097	-0.002	3.097	0.000
19	3.013	0.017	3.015	0.004	3.016	-0.002	3.016	0.000
19.5	2.936	0.015	2.938	0.004	2.939	-0.002	2.938	0.000
20	2.862	0.014	2.864	0.004	2.865	-0.002	2.865	0.000

Switch Sleepers

The following table is used by Trax to determine the number of sleepers placed under switch blades of a certain length or type. The first is placed with its centre line 4" forward (i.e. towards the heel) of the switch blade ends, and the last is placed 1' 1" back from the joint (old-type switches) or first 'fixed' chair (flexible switches). The switches are spaced equidistantly.

Switch Type	Number of Sleepers	Switch type	Number of Sleepers
9ft old-type	4	A type flexible	8
10ft old-type	5	B type flexible	10
12ft old-type	6	C type flexible	12
14ft old-type	7	D type flexible	13
15ft old-type	7		
16ft old-type	8		
18ft old-type	9		
20ft old-type	10		
30ft old-type	14		

Wing and Check Rails

Trax determines the length of wing and check rails according to the crossing angle of the crossing they are protecting. For a crossing angle, N, the lengths used are given in the table below. The wing length is from knuckle to the start of the splayed end of the wing rail. The check rail length includes the two splayed ends.

N	Wing	Splay	Check
below 7	2ft 6ins	3ft 6ins	11ft 6ins
7 to 7^1/$_2$	3ft	3ft 6ins	11ft 6ins
8 to 9	3ft	3ft 6ins	13ft 6ins
9^1/$_2$ to 10	3ft 6ins	3ft 6ins	13ft 6ins
10^1/$_2$ to 11	4ft	3ft	13ft 6ins
11^1/$_2$ to 12	4ft	3ft	16ft
12^1/$_2$ to 13^1/$_2$	4ft 6ins	2ft 6ins	16ft
14 and over	5ft	2ft 6ins	16ft

These values are reasonably typical, however for exact dimensions for a particular railway, you will need to consult specialist literature such as *GWR Switch and Crossing Practice* by David J Smith (published by The Great Western Study Group) or *British Railway Track, Design, Construction and Maintenance*, edited by C.L.Heeler (published by the Permanent Way Institution).

Suppliers of Parts and Materials

The following is a list of suppliers of whom the authors have heard, or with whom they have dealt. It is by no means claimed as an exhaustive list, but is merely a result our experience in building track over a number of years. Any omissions should not be taken to imply anything other than that the authors have not heard of a particular supplier.

C & L Finescale Ltd.
Cadbury Camp Lane, Clapton in Gordano, BS20 7SD. *Rail, sleepers, chairs, switch blades, crossing vees, templates, etc for chaired construction in 4mm and 7mm scales.*

Charles Cantrill Ltd
Carver Street, Birmingham, West Midlands, B1 3AN. *Quality Cork Supplies. Cork in sheets, rolls and granules for trackwork and scenic display.*

Exactoscale Ltd
29 Couchmore Avenue, Esher KT10 9AS. *Rail, chairs, sleepers, fishplates etc. templates, jigs and clamps for chaired construction. 4mm and 7mm scales.*

Marcway
598-600 Attercliffe Rd, Sheffield S9 3QS. *Rail, sleeper strip, etc for copperclad construction. Also ready-made pointwork in 7mm and 10mm scales.*

Masokits Masterbits Range
27 Crotch Crescent, New Marston, Oxford, Oxfordshire, OX3 0JL *Etched chairs, point tiebars and cranks in 4mm.*

Modeloils
12 Marina Drive, Wolverton, Buckinghamshire, MK12 5DW. *'Slippery Sid' wire-in-tube mechanical signal and point operating system for all scales.*

Peco (Pritchard Patent Product Co Ltd)
Beer, Seaton, Devon, EX12 3NA. *Ready built trackwork in 2mm, 4mm, 7mm and other scales.*

Railwood Products
30 Frilsham Way, Coventry, CV5 9LH. *Steel radius curves from 3' to 60', also straights.*

"Red Dog"
9 Harcourt, Bradwell, Milton Keynes, MK13 9EN. *Useful selection of metalwork bits and pieces for baseboard construction.*

SMP
1B St Johns, Warwick, Warwickshire, CV34 4NE. *Components for copperclad track and point construction in 4mm scale.*

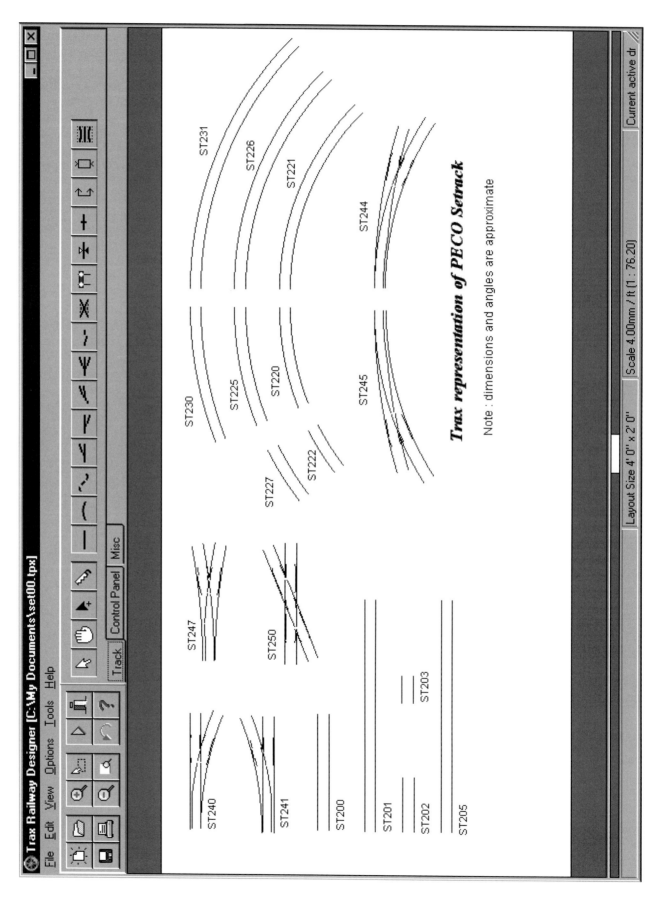

Trax representation of PECO Setrack

Note : dimensions and angles are approximate

Representing ready-made track using *Trax*

Many users of *Trax* have requested the facility to represent ready-made track, such as that supplied by PECO, on a *Trax* layout. With *Trax 2*, therefore, we have introduced a facility to 'import' a file of pre-prepared points and crossings. These may then be copied and pasted as many times as are required, then joined up in the usual way. You can also create your own library of pre-prepared track part files for inclusion in your future layouts.

The files you import into a layout are distinguished from normal *Trax* files by having the file extension 'tpx' rather than the normal 'trx'. There are one or two rules you must observe in using these. First, the file you import must use the same scale, gauge, flangeway, track interval etc as that of your main layout - otherwise the trackwork would be incompatible. Second, when you import a file it's contents (the track parts) are displayed in their locations *as they were originally exported*. This might mean they overwrite some of your layout. Therefore, it is a good idea to import your parts file first, before you start inserting parts of your own.

On your CD, look for files with the 'tpx' extension. These are the ones you can import into your layout. For example, the file *set00.tpx* contains a *Trax* representation of the Peco Setrack 00 range. It must be emphasised that this representation is not exact, however. The Peco track geometry differs in some subtle ways from that employed by *Trax*. Therefore, when *Trax* draws certain parts, there are small dimensional differences. Straights and curves are exact, as are the standard right and left hand points (ST240 and ST241) with the track interval set to 67mm. The diamond crossing, however, is represented as a 1 in 2½ crossing by *Trax*, giving it a crossing angle of 22.918°. The Peco crossing has an angle of 22.5°, which is slightly different. Also, the curved points (ST244 and ST245) have a slightly different geometry. *Trax* gives curved points a constant radius through each of the two curves, whereas the Peco points do not have a constant radius. Therefore, the *Trax* representation is not exactly the same.

Despite these differences, however, the 'import' facility will give you the ability to design a close approximation (within a millimetre or two) to a Peco-based layout. This should be more than adequate to allow you to test out the main operational issues such as electrics, overall dimensions etc. The file *geometry.trx* contains a Setrack layout (in fact, the one used to illustrate Setrack geometry in the Peco Setrack Templates leaflet) which you can experiment with to see how the electrics etc. work.

To illustrate the use of import files, you can follow the step below. This will also give new users an insight into some of the *Trax* facilities.

Step 1

Open the *Trax* program, and from the File menu, select New. You could also use the keyboard shortcut (Ctrl + N) or click the 'New Layout' Toolbutton on the top left of the *Trax* window. Any of these will bring up the 'New Layout' dialog box. On the dialog box, you will find the places to enter your layout size, modelling scale etc. For reasons that will become apparent later, make the width of your layout around twice the size you actually want it. This will give us space to move things around. Set the modelling scale to '00 gauge 4mm/ft' and note that this will automatically set the other dimensions to appropriate values (track gauge, etc). The one thing you will need to change is the 'Interval between tracks', which you should set to 67mm, this being the Setrack standard. By the way, if you will always want to use the same scale and gauge, click the 'Save as default' button, and this will be saved as the starting screen every time you create a new layout. Click OK, and *Trax* will set up a new layout for you.

Step 2

Go to the File menu again, and select Import. This will bring up the File Open dialog box. Browse to find the *set00.tpx* file, which should normally be in your *Trax* directory if you used the standard installation procedure. Click Open, and you should see an example of each of the Setrack items illustrated with its name (ST200, etc). The items will be on the left hand side of the layout. We want to move them over to the right, as we will be building our own layout on the left. If there is insufficient space for these and about the same area again, go to the Edit menu, and select Layout Settings. You will note that this brings back memories of the 'New Layout' dialog box. In fact, it is the same box except that we cannot now change things like the scale, gauge etc. This is because we now have track parts on the layout, and *Trax* will not allow us to mix two different scales. It will, however, allow us to change the layout size. Do this if required and click OK.

Step 3

Having got space to move the Setrack samples into, select the Move tool by clicking the 'hand' button on the 'Track' palette. Then, go to the Edit menu and click Select All Layout. You will notice that all of the parts change to the highlight colour. Now, the next step has to be exactly right. Press and hold down the Ctrl key on your keyboard, move the mouse cursor (now a hand) until its hotspot (the fingertips) is between the rails of one of the track parts, and with the Ctrl button still held down, click down the left hand mouse button, drag the mouse to the position to which you want to move the selected parts then release the mouse button. Finally, release the Ctrl button. The reason you have to do things in this order is that, when you select something to move with the hand tool, this normally deselects all previously selected parts. Only if you hold down Ctrl can you keep the current

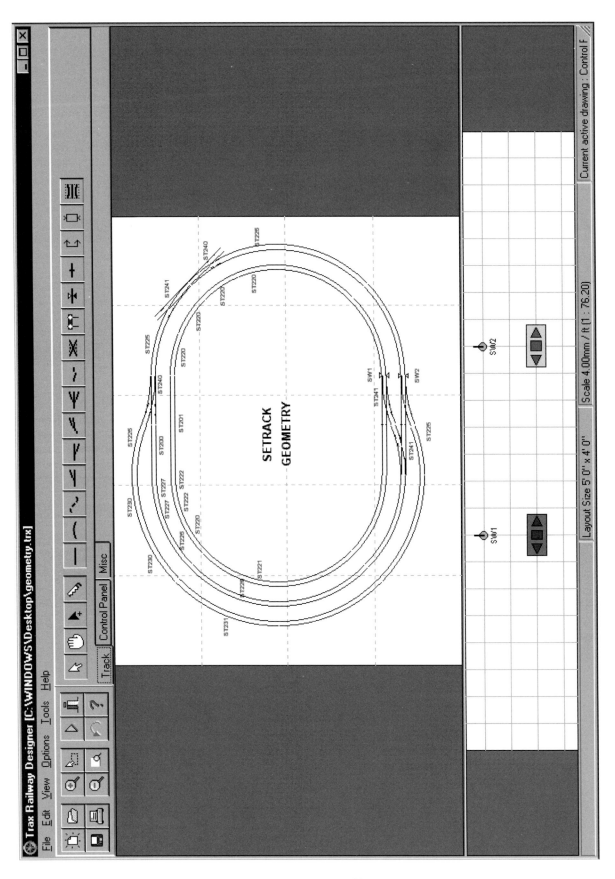

selection. Once you have enough space on the left to build your layout, get rid of the hand cursor by clicking the 'select' button (an arrow).

Step 4

Select a right-hand point (ST240) by clicking between its rails with the mouse cursor. Once selected, it will be highlighted. Now, from the Edit menu select Copy Selected Parts. This will place a copy of the ST240 on the Windows clipboard. Now select Paste from the edit menu, and note that the mouse cursor now has a little box attached to it, to represent the fact that there is something available to be added to the layout. Pick a spot somewhere in the left of the layout, click the left mouse button and you will have a copy of the point. Click it again in a slightly different location, and you should get another copy.

Step 5

Repeat the actions of *step 4,* but this time use a medium-length straight (ST200). You should now have two right hand points and two straights ready to join up. Select the joining tool by clicking the button with the black arrow and a '+' sign on the Track palette. Now, join the two points together at their 'turnout' ends. Click first on one of the points close to the end of the curved turnout, again taking care to click between the rails. Note that it is highlighted, and also there is a small cross at the selected end. This marks the end we are going to join up to. Now click the other ST240 in the same area. If you get this right, the second point should 'jump' and join itself onto the first, with their two curved turnout tracks connected.

Step 6

Now, in a similar manner, join up the two ST200 straights to the 'toe' ends of the two points (see figure 2.5), and you should have a perfect double track facing crossover. If you make a mistake, you can correct it, but only if you *immediately* select Edit, Undo (or click the Undo button on the toolbar). If you do other things in between times, you will not be able to do this. A common mistake when joining parts is to forget the rule that it is the first part you click that stays put and the second part that moves to join it. Note also that if you now move one of the joined parts using the hand tool, all of them move. In effect, they are now a single unit.

Step 7

You can now copy and paste curves and straights to make up a double track oval with your crossover in one side. You will need to paste 8 copies of ST231, and 8 of ST226, to make up the semicircles, then 4 copies of ST200 to join them at the opposite side of your oval from the crossover. It is a good idea to save your work at regular intervals, which you can do by selecting Save from the File menu, or using the keyboard shortcut Ctrl + S, or simply clicking the save button on the toolbar. Select a suitable name for your file, and *Trax* will save it for you.

Step 8

Once you have used all the parts you need from the Setrack templates, you can delete them. The quickest way to do this is to use the Select Tool (an arrow on the Track palette). Click a part, then press the Del key on your keyboard and it will disappear.

Once the unwanted Setrack parts have gone, you can make the layout smaller. Remember we made it larger than required at the beginning in order to fit in the import file and our own track plan. From the Edit menu, select Layout Settings, and adjust the size accordingly. When you have finished, your work should resemble the file *example.trx* on your CD. Note that this has had track feeds and breaks added so that you can test the electrics for shorts etc. The electrical capabilities of Trax are outside the scope of this book, but you can find out all about them in *Wiring the Layout* (KRB Publications).

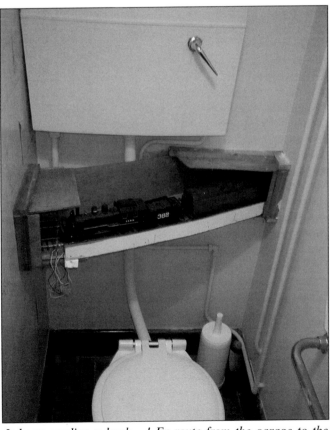

It beats reading a book.....! En-route from the garage to the garden, Philip Morgan's American based line has to traverse the smallest room. A suitable 'covered way' was thus provided - to guard against any customer embarrassment. It is photographed here with the cover temporarily removed.